of God's Presence

on the Road Ahead

no matter what,

no matter where

L A R R Y   L I B B Y   &

S T E V E   H A L L I D A Y

WaterBrook
P R E S S

No Matter What, No Matter Where
Published by WaterBrook Press
5446 North Academy Boulevard, Suite 200
Colorado Springs, Colorado 80918
A division of Random House, Inc.

ISBN 1-57856-314-3

Library of Congress Cataloging-in-Publication Data
Libby, Larry.
    No matter what, no matter where : the promise of God's presence on the road ahead /
by Larry Libby and Steve Halliday.—1st ed.
        p.   cm.
    Includes bibliographical references.
    ISBN 1-57856-314-3
    1. Christian life.   2. Presence of God.   I. Halliday, Steve, 1957–   II. Title.
BV4509.5 L5355 2000
242—dc21   99-088476

Printed in the United States of America
2000—First Edition

10 9 8 7 6 5 4 3 2 1

For my two wonderful teenagers,
Matthew & Melissa

May God's mighty Son, our faithful Lord and Shepherd,
light your way and remain your Best Friend forever.
Love, Dad
—L.L.

contents

Introduction: What Have We Here? *1*

1. He Knows Me
   God understands me perfectly *3*

2. Past, Present, and Future
   He surrounds me with His love *14*

3. A Never-Ending Wonder
   My life has an eternal dimension *25*

4. Global Positioning
   He is with me everywhere *34*

5. A Hand in the Dark
   He guides me and holds me close *43*

6. A Sure and Steady Light
   He shines His light on times of confusion *52*

7. Manufacturer's Guarantee
   He made me the way I am *62*

8. No Wasted Days
   He has a plan for me *72*

9. Always on His Mind
   I am continually in His thoughts *82*

10. The End Game for Evil
    He will right every wrong *92*

11. The Most Important Thing in the World
    Yielding my will to His *103*

12. Trailhead to Eternity
    In search of the "way everlasting" *113*

what have we here?

Books written for those just starting out on a new phase of life typically offer flowery words, inspirational quotes, and impassioned calls for you to "realize your potential."

This one doesn't.

Books of this sort traditionally tell you that the sky is your limit, that humankind can achieve anything it sets its mind to, and that your success will depend on dreaming big dreams and pursuing your goals with diligence.

This one won't.

This is basically a book about one of the most amazing songs ever written, by one of the most unique poets who ever lived.

What's so special about a song written over four thousand years ago by a Jewish shepherd named David? Just this: Many of those who have taken time to ponder Psalm 139 feel as though David somehow reached below the busyness of life to touch something breathtakingly deep, where thoughts seldom reach.

Go-get-'em quotes, you-can-do-it cards from Hallmark, and rah-rah, locker-room speeches will take you only so far—maybe into the

1

next hour, the next day, or the next week. But these words of David will take you beyond time into eternity. If what he writes is true (and we believe every word), there is Someone out there who knows you better than you know yourself—Someone who cares profoundly about every detail of your life, Someone who will place a hand on your shoulder and guide you into the best and brightest prospects for your life, *beginning today.*

As the authors of this book, we have taken turns placing different sections of this psalm under the spotlight. Along the way we've taken time to reveal a bit of our own journey, as we have come to grips with some startling truths. (You'll see Steve Halliday's initials following some of the chapters, and Larry Libby's initials following others.)

These twenty-four verses contain so much that we can't help feeling we need to say more. But we didn't. (That's another thing about books like these. They're short!) We picked up only a few golden pebbles from the surface of the ground, while vast deposits of truth wait to be mined below.

Still, they are pebbles worth keeping—worth carrying around in your pocket for the next seventy years or so. What we've found, we're happy to pass along in these few pages. Please know that our prayers for God's best in your life come bound with this book.

he knows me

God understands me perfectly

O LORD, you have searched me
 and you know me.
You know when I sit and when I rise;
 you perceive my thoughts from afar.
You discern my going out and my lying down;
 you are familiar with all my ways.
Before a word is on my tongue
 you know it completely, O LORD.

PSALM 139:1-4

I'll never forget what happened my senior year at my high school's yearbook signing party. Boni, one of the class clowns, made some predictably clever comment and shoved her yearbook at me.

Sometimes it's a chore to know what to say. The same old clichés? Something funny? Something serious? Trouble was, I really didn't know Boni, other than being in a couple of school plays with her. In

Thornton Wilder's *The Skin of Our Teeth,* I had played the part of Henry Antrobus (the sort of "angry young man" role I relished). Boni played a wild and crazy go-go girl.

Even though her name was pronounced "Bonnie," people called her "Bone-y" or "Bones" because she was so thin. A self-described "loudmouth," she seemed to enjoy dressing and behaving in an off-beat, wacky sort of way, walking the edge between acceptable behavior and throwing the director into a tizzy fit. Had she been in high school today, I suppose she would have dyed her hair some vivid shade of purple.

What could I write? "Keep being crazy, Bones. Never change." Or maybe, "Wasn't it a blast in Mr. Daw's class?"

Suddenly I didn't want to write that kind of twaddle. I knew that I would probably never see this girl again, and for some reason I felt like contributing something more than a throwaway line. I had the feeling there was more to her than met the eye, that behind all her outrageous behavior and cutting up there was, well, someone else. Someone shy and thoughtful—but terribly afraid of being ignored. She had found "acceptance" and a niche in high school as the clown, the funny girl. Was she trapped by that role? If she ever said anything thoughtful, the kids laughed it off. No one took her seriously.

On a whim I chose to write to that "other" Boni, knowing I might be grossly wide of the mark (but sensing I wasn't). I said something like this: "Everyone knows one Boni. The funny, wild kid. The crazy go-go girl in the miniskirt. I see another Boni. Someone with a tender heart who cares a lot about people. Someone with dreams and hopes no one else knows about. A quieter, more thoughtful Boni. I'm glad I got to know the one; wish there had been time to meet the other."

It was really a stab in the dark. I could have been laughed at (about the worst thing that can happen to a high school guy), scorned for playing amateur psychologist. She could have blown it off with a joke and a chuckle and made me feel like an idiot.

But she didn't.

Later in the party the "other" Boni came over to talk to me. I was surprised to see her eyes full of tears. She just looked at me for a moment or two before speaking.

"No one has ever said anything like that to me," she said softly. "How…how did you know? That was the most wonderful thing you could have said."

With that, she gave me a quick, shy hug and hurried away. And after that night, I never saw her again.

What moved Boni's heart so deeply? What made her value those few lines of blue ink in the corner of a page in her yearbook? I think it was that someone made an effort, however clumsy, to truly understand her. In my case it was mostly a lucky guess—coupled, perhaps, with a rare flash of intuition. But she treasured it all the same.

In God's case, however, there is no guesswork. Nor does He experience "flashes" of insight. He doesn't know things intuitively; He simply *knows*.

THE WAYS THAT HE KNOWS ME

Could it really be that God knows *everything* about us? That was certainly David's conviction. I picture him as a young shepherd, sitting at twilight on a grassy slope, plucking his harp as his flock grazes in the gathering darkness. David wrote songs, and if he lived today, he might dominate the pop charts, direct the Israel Philharmonic, or take Nashville by storm (terrible thought!). He composed hundreds of songs and hymns, expressing in them a kaleidoscope of emotions and experiences. He became known in his own time as "the sweet psalmist of Israel" (2 Samuel 23:1, KJV).

On the night he wrote this song, the ballad we know by the bland title of "Psalm 139," I imagine him looking off toward the evening star, shining like molten silver on the horizon. With all the immensity of space before him, the stars blinking on one by one in the measureless heavens, it seized David with wonder to think of a God who *knew him.* He sang as his fingers caressed the strings,

> *O LORD, you have searched me*
> *and you know me.*

The word David used for "know" reflects a deep, intimate knowledge. It's something more than "knowing" the chemistry formulas for a quiz. It would be more like getting inside the actual chemical reactions! In fact, the word David employed is the very same one used for sexual relations, as when the Bible says Adam "knew" his wife, Eve.

When David wrote Psalm 139, he knew he could pour out the full contents of his soul to God and always be fully understood, for God *knew* David. I think that thought filled the young man with awe. At that point in his life, virtually *no one* knew him, and those who did weren't inclined toward a good opinion. How well did his own brothers know him? Not very well! They were all too quick to accuse him of neglecting his duties or grandstanding to get attention. In one account, we read:

> But when David's oldest brother, Eliab, heard David
> talking like that, he was angry. "What are you doing
> around here, anyway?" he demanded. "What about the
> sheep you're supposed to be taking care of? I know what
> a cocky brat you are; you just want to see the battle!"
> (1 Samuel 17:28, TLB)

Cocky brat? What a classic line! That has to be right out of the *Big Brother's Handbook.* The fact is, David's family really didn't know his heart at all. His own father, Jesse, thought him so insignificant he didn't even bring him into the house with the rest of the family to meet a distinguished guest. (See 1 Samuel 16.)

David's eventual employer, King Saul, looked at him with distrust and suspicion almost from day one. Later his future wife would misread his zeal and mock him for lacking kingly dignity.

But *the Lord* knew him. Knew his heart. Knew his motives. Knew his dreams. Knew the bone-deep longings David could hardly frame into words.

How thoroughly did He know him? The young shepherd's song went on:

You know when I sit and when I rise;
you perceive my thoughts from afar.

In other words, even before David's musings had crystallized, even while they were still forming under pools of conscious thought, God knew what they would be and where they would lead. With such knowledge—and David's cooperation—God's Spirit could turn his mind along thought trails that consistently pleased and honored Him. But David wasn't finished yet.

Before a word is on my tongue
you know it completely, O LORD.

The God of Israel knew David so totally, so exhaustively, that He knew precisely what the psalmist would say long before the syllables formed on his lips. That's comforting for someone like me, because I don't always get the chance to vocalize those syllables.

He Knows Where I'm Going

Are you a person who has difficulty holding your own in a conversation? For some reason I've never been much good at it. By the time I've thought of something relevant or witty to add to the dialogue, the train has already zipped by, and I'm left standing by the empty tracks.

If I do succeed in gaining the floor, I will sometimes see people's eyes begin to wander as I'm baring my soul. If I ever had their attention, I let it slip away from me. My thoughts can form so s-l-o-w-l-y! It's a speech habit that drives other people nuts.

I don't know why I do it. It's just a quirk of the microprocessor lodged between my ears. Here's what happens. I begin a sentence, think about it while I'm speaking, and pause just a second or two before I finish. I'll say, for instance, "I don't eat many doughnuts these days…[pause for a two-count]…because my favorite bakery closed down."

Before I can get to the part about the bakery, someone will jump in to "help me out," as though we had been playing twenty questions.

"…because you've been putting on weight."

"…because you don't want to LOOK like a doughnut."

"…because doughnuts are loaded with fat and sugar."

Just because so many other people are wired at 300 MHz and I plug along at 50, it doesn't mean I dislike finishing my own sentences. Sometimes the contributions from my impatient friends are better than what I want to say, so I just let them run with it. At other times, they are the *opposite* of what I intended, and I have to protest: "Wait a minute. That's not where I was going at all!"

Yet God knows where I'm going before I ever open my mouth. He knows exactly what I mean and why I said it. "Word choice" in my prayers doesn't matter to Him because He considers the heart behind the words. It doesn't matter if I pause five minutes in the middle of a sentence—or don't even finish the thought. He knows what I want to say when I can't find the words. He knows what I want to sing when I can't find the tune.

And God knows you. He has the full story. He has studied every line—and between the lines. He understands you better than anyone else ever will or ever could. That is a comforting thing to remember when others so dreadfully misunderstand you. And make no mistake, they will. Believe me, I know.

THE WRONG THING AT THE WRONG TIME

I said it. It came out of my mouth, and I reaped the consequences. *Fast.*

Hardly more than a rookie book editor at the time, I had been asked to phone a highly respected pastor and author and confirm some details about an upcoming book. That seemed simple enough, but somehow, in the course of our conversation, I said *something* (I still don't know what it was) that triggered this good man's indignation and anger. Almost immediately I could feel the receiver heat up next to my ear. He'd had it "up to here" with so-called Christian publishers who were out only to make a buck. *Where* was our integrity? *Where* was our honesty? *Where* was our compassion? Did we care so little about the eternal destiny of men and women or for the reputation of our Lord?

Ouch! There was no stopping him. I could tell frustration had been building for years, and all it took was one spark to ignite the highly flammable contents—a spark that inadvertently fell from my mouth. Suddenly I, Larry Libby, novice editor for a Bible-school publishing house, became the focal point for all the commercialization, trivialization, abuses, hypocrisy, and moneygrubbing greed that could be found in the whole religious publishing industry.

The man's wrath grew mighty, and I had to endure the storm. What really hurt was that I so admired and respected this seasoned Christian warrior. He was a hero. This was like being ripped into by Moses or Saint Peter! Much of what he said was right, and yet it really had nothing to do with *me*. I hadn't done any of those things. I was simply trying to make conversation and inadvertently said something that touched him off. How could he assign such terrible motives to me, someone he'd hardly even met?

When I put down the phone, tears stung the edges of my eyes and a lump the size of a golf ball wedged somewhere near my larynx. Man! It *hurts* to be misunderstood. Few things in life wound and frustrate more than being misread, misquoted, or misinterpreted.

Have you ever known the sting of being misunderstood? Perhaps you didn't choose the course of study that someone thought you should, or maybe you're on a career track that has raised a few eyebrows. Those folks didn't understand what you did, and they let you know of their disapproval.

But God *never* misunderstands. Never gets a faulty idea. Never misconstrues a word you say or a thought you entertain. He understands you better than you understand yourself. Especially when your thoughts grow jumbled and confused.

When Words Won't Come

In Romans 8, Paul writes about times of deep distress, when you're gripped with fear or swamped with depression *and no words will come.* You may feel a desperate need for God. You long for His help, His wisdom, His nearness, His forgiveness—but somehow you just don't have it in you to call to Him. All you can do is shoot a quick glance toward heaven and sigh—or groan within yourself.

It's like that for a lot of us when we're just starting out on some new adventure. The journey ahead excites us, but it scares us a little too. We might wish to ask God for wisdom or for any one of a thousand other things, but the words just won't come.

In that very moment, the Bible says, heaven gets the full message! God gets a complete readout of what you want, what you need, what you fear, what you regret, what puzzles you greatly, and what you long for with all your heart.

Paul says it like this:

> In the same way, the Spirit helps us in our weakness. We do not know what we ought to pray for, but the Spirit himself intercedes for us with groans that words cannot express. And he who searches our hearts knows the mind of the Spirit, because the Spirit intercedes for the saints in accordance with God's will. (Romans 8:26-27)

In other words, don't worry about the "right" words! Just look up to your heavenly Father and invite Him to read your heart. Quick as a blink, you will find yourself in the middle of profound, intimate contact with the best friend you will ever have in time or eternity.

Others may misunderstand you or misread your motives. Not Him! Others may believe the actor in you that keeps playing a part you don't even like. He knows better. Others may not take the time to get to know you. But God knows you already and delights in your company. Before you even open your mouth, you have His full attention.

And you always will.

—L.L.

past, present, and future

He surrounds me with His love

You hem me in—behind and before;
you have laid your hand upon me.

PSALM 139:5

What am I doing here?

I kept asking that question as I lay shivering in my flimsy sleeping bag. A nearly full moon cast a soft light inside the tent, but what comfort was that? Not that *Mark* was having any trouble getting to sleep. My friend seemed to fall into dreamland almost as soon as he went horizontal. Neither the cold, stony ground beneath us nor the nip in the air of an early fall evening in the Boundary Waters Canoe Area seemed able to keep him awake ten seconds after he shut his eyes.

My mind went back to the conversations between my mom and me just days before. She had strongly opposed this trip. She didn't think it wise for two semiexperienced campers, just out of high school, to trek alone into the Minnesota northwoods to spend ten days at isolated Wolf Lake, many hours from civilization (and medical help). But I insisted. I was a grownup now. We could take care of ourselves.

What am I doing here? I honestly couldn't tell what was most responsible for keeping me awake: my chattering teeth, the fresh bear tracks we had just discovered near our camp site, the wolves howling at the moon on the other side of the lake, or the loaded shotgun Mark insisted on taking to bed with him.

I felt many things on that trip, but "safe" wasn't one of them. Still, beyond the sleepless nights and that unfortunate incident at the end of our adventure, when we capsized our canoe—we ended up walking several hundred yards through a muddy bog full of sharp reeds, towing our half-submerged boat and its waterlogged cargo—we made it through unscathed. Even though it didn't enter our minds at the time, God was busy watching over us. Any one of our stupid decisions could have cost us more than we were prepared to pay, but God in His mercy saw to it that we lost nothing but some shuteye and a good deal of impudence.

We thought we had struck out on our own, but of course we hadn't. God went with us all the way. As David had written millennia earlier,

> *You hem me in—behind and before;*
> *you have laid your hand upon me.*

Even in the wilds of northern Minnesota, our Lord had hedged us in for the purpose of protection. His omnipotent hand covered us, guided us, and held us close. That's a splendid truth to remember whenever we strike out "on our own."

HEMMED IN!

David uses an unlikely word when he declares to God, "You hem me in." The Hebrew term *surl,* translated here as "hem in," is used some thirty-five times in the Old Testament, and in every other instance it carries the meaning "to besiege" or "to enclose," as when an invading army lays siege to a city. In 2 Samuel 20:15, for example, the Bible says, "All the troops with Joab came and besieged *(surl)* Sheba in Abel Beth Maacah. They built a siege ramp up to the city, and it stood against the outer fortifications. While they were battering the wall to bring it down…"

Do you see why it seems an unlikely word to bring comfort? Siege ramps, battering rams, famine, terror, war—where is the encouragement in that?

But David, old warrior that he was, found great assurance in this unusual word picture. In his mind's eye he imagined almighty God completely surrounding him, enveloping him so totally with angelic warriors and heavenly implements of war that nothing—not a rat, not a flea, not even a breath of foul air—could penetrate the divine circle. No matter where David looked, he saw God "hemming him in"—but not for destruction!

Here is where the soldier-king "flipped" the image in his mind. God and His celestial armies had encircled David, not to harm him but to protect him. They had dug in to the east and west and south and north, not to overthrow the king but to uphold him, to defend him, to bless him. David saw himself "hemmed in," not by an enemy but by an omnipotent Protector and Friend.

Elsewhere in the Psalms this same theme is reiterated and enlarged:

> For surely, O LORD, you bless the righteous;
> you surround them with your favor as with
> a shield. (5:12)

> The angel of the LORD encamps around those
> who fear him,
> and he delivers them. (34:7)

> As the mountains surround Jerusalem,
> so the LORD surrounds his people
> both now and forevermore. (125:2)

The patriarch Job enjoyed similar protection. At the beginning of the book of Job, the Lord is "bragging" on his servant, calling Satan's attention to Job's integrity and piety. The devil replies, "Have you not put a hedge around him and his household and everything he has? You have blessed the work of his hands, so that his flocks and herds are spread throughout the land" (Job 1:10).

What an encouragement to know the Lord hems us in and erects a hedge of protection around us! Yet as amazing as this is, the picture doesn't stop there. For David doesn't have in mind only geographical protection, but temporal protection as well. He sees God hemming him in not only in space but in *time*.

When David wrote in Psalm 139:4, "Before a word is on my tongue you know it completely, O LORD," he implied that God knew every detail about his future. And when he said in verse 16, "All the days ordained for me were written in your book before one of them came to be," he declared the truth emphatically. He rejoiced that God "hemmed him in" through all the days to come.

And even when he looked at the sands of time already fallen through the hourglass, David saw God's protection. He exulted that long before he was born, God saw his "unformed body" (verse 16). Think of it! Even before a thought appeared in David's head, God was protecting him, hemming him in. God's special protection extends from the present into the future; in fact, from before David was born until…well, there is no "until." God will hem David in through all eternity!

And He will do the same for you.

A CASE STUDY

What does it mean for you and me to be "hemmed in" by a divine Protector and Friend? Will we be excused from hardship and pain and disappointment? Will our ship always sail in fair winds and never fail to reach our planned destination on schedule?

Well…no.

The apostle Paul believed, as did David, that God hemmed him in, both behind and before. He knew he had been chosen to proclaim the Good News of Jesus Christ to whomever would listen, whether Jew or Gentile. Yet from the very beginning of his ministry, God let him know how much he would suffer for the Lord's name (Acts 9:16). The book of Acts and Paul's own letters chronicle the severe nature of that suffering: beatings, floggings, imprisonment, a stoning, ship-wrecks, hunger, exposure.

Yet despite all of it, God "hemmed him in." When Paul visited Corinth and certain "Jews opposed Paul and became abusive" (Acts 18:6), Luke tells us that "one night the Lord spoke to Paul in a vision: 'Do not be afraid; keep on speaking, do not be silent. For I am with you, and no one is going to attack and harm you, because I have many people in this city'" (verses 9-10).

Later, while sailing to Rome after his arrest in Jerusalem for preaching the gospel, a storm of hurricane force called a "northeaster" pummeled his ship and crewmates for two weeks, until they lost all hope of being saved. But during the worst part of the storm, an angel of God stood beside Paul and said, "Do not be afraid, Paul. You must stand trial before Caesar; and God has graciously given you the lives of all who sail with you" (Acts 27:24).

God would allow nothing to cut short His plans for Paul. He was "hemming him in" for the purpose of protection.

But don't think this divine "hemming in" kicks into gear only when danger arises! Paul's missionary travels demonstrate that God often *changes the direction of our lives* by "hemming us in." It's one of the methods He uses to guide us.

In Acts 16 Paul and Silas and their team apparently planned to preach the word "in the province of Asia," but Luke says they were "kept by the Holy Spirit" from doing so (verse 6).

In other words, they were hemmed in.

Next they tried to enter Bithynia, "but the Spirit of Jesus would not allow them to" (verse 7). How? We don't know. But it was another hemming in.

No doubt Paul and his team now felt great disappointment. To be kept twice from proclaiming the glory of God to those who had never heard the message of Christ? What could God be up to? Perhaps they felt like the young man whose college application is rejected by the only school he ever wanted to attend. Maybe their hearts burned with the same sadness felt by the young woman who is passed over for the dream job she'd fantasized about for years. To be hemmed in doesn't always *feel* like a blessing.

But when God is the one at work, it really is. In Paul's case, an unexpected night vision convinced him that he and his team ought to leave immediately for Macedonia to preach the gospel there. And so they arrived exactly where God wanted them; He hemmed them in until they reached the very area He had chosen for them. And on that day their joy exploded.

Aren't you glad for God's hemming in? By it He protects us, and through it He guides us. And perhaps the best thing of all is this: when God hems us in, He doesn't do so through some heavenly bureaucrat or an earthly subcontractor. He does it personally, one-to-one. In the Bible's language, He does it with His own hand.

THE TOUCH OF GOD

"You have laid your hand upon me," said David to God. Now, when someone lays a hand on you, it can be either a good thing or a bad thing. It is *not* a good thing when your mother says to you, "Wait until your father comes home and lays his hands on you!" (I can vouch for that.) It was *not* a good thing when Nehemiah said to some merchants who were violating the Sabbath, "Why do you spend the night by the wall? If you do this again, I will lay hands on you" (Nehemiah 13:21).

But in Psalm 139, the hand in David's mind is gentle, friendly, strong, and encouraging. Perhaps he was thinking of old Jacob, who tenderly placed his gnarled hands on the heads of Joseph's two sons to bless them (Genesis 48:10-20). Or maybe he was picturing how the Lord lovingly placed Moses in the cleft of a rock and covered him with His hand when the prophet asked to see the divine glory (Exodus 33:12-23). What is certain is that the shepherd-king looked for compassionate and firm hands to hem him in. David expected God Himself to place His hands on him.

What a marvel this is! There is something intensely personal and intimate about a caring touch. Have you ever noticed how often Jesus chose to heal the sick with a touch? Of course He didn't need to make physical contact. He could have cured any disease or repaired any injury with a single word. Sometimes He did just that (Matthew 8:13; 15:28). He spoke, and from a great distance away, the sick were healed.

But far more often the Master "reached out his hand and

touched" the sufferer (Matthew 8:3), deliberately placing his hands even on an "untouchable" leper. He "took the blind man by the hand" and "put his hands on him" to restore his sight (Mark 8:23). He "took the children in his arms, put his hands on them and blessed them" (Mark 10:16).

The Touch That Lingers

Why this insistence on touching? Why this compulsion to place a hand on the body of another? What's so significant about physical contact?

In the past few years I have come to understand better the enormous significance of touch. In my family, shaped by its Scandinavian heritage, warm touch (especially among men) wasn't a big part of the landscape. I knew I was loved and I have wonderful memories of my growing up years, full of fun and acceptance and encouragement. It's just that there wasn't a lot of touch between my dad and me. He communicated his bountiful love in other ways.

But something changed a few years ago. I'll never forget the first time I visited Mom and Dad after my father became a Christian (he didn't accept Christ into his life until long after all of his four children had left home). Now, my dad's character didn't need to change much once he came to faith. He had always been a responsible, self-controlled, good-hearted man whom everyone liked and admired. In fact, I think that was part of the reason he took so long to join God's family. He didn't see the need! He looked at men in the church and thought, *Hey, I'm at least that good.* And he was probably right.

So when I returned home that first time, I didn't notice many changes in my dad's language or dress or habits. It did startle me when it was my *dad* who said, "Let's pray" at the dinner table. I'd never heard that before! But that isn't what moved me most profoundly.

What really stunned me, what will stick in my memory forever, is what happened at the airport. In all the years past, when it was time to leave, I had given my mom a big hug and my dad a firm handshake. But when I turned to grasp Dad's hand, my reserved, formerly un-touchy father reached his burly arms around my torso and gave me a great bear hug. Nothing flashy. And not long—no more than a second or two.

But in that remarkable moment, a strange tingling sensation spread over my body, and I knew that he loved me, as much as I knew my name was Steven William Halliday. I don't believe my face registered the surprise that shook my soul, and just moments later I was walking alone down the jetway to board my plane. But that tingling sensation wouldn't go away.

I had been touched! Touched in a way I hadn't expected. Touched in a way that assured me I was loved, cherished, and missed. Touched in a way that connected me to my father as never before.

Several years have passed since that tender airport farewell, and many times I've returned home to visit my parents. Each time now I get hugs from both Mom and Dad.

I like it.

God likes it too. That's why He built us with a desire to touch and be touched, and that's why He's so fond of laying His hands on us. It's no accident that in one of the Bible's final pictures of God, it is declared that "now the dwelling of God is with men, and he will live with them. They will be his people, and God himself will be with them and be their God. *He will wipe every tear from their eyes*" (Revelation 21:3-4, emphasis added).

How? With a touch. A glorious, gentle touch. For the omnipotent hands that hem us in are also the loving hands that long to gently embrace us.

—*S.H.*

a never-ending wonder

My life has an eternal dimension

Such knowledge is too wonderful for me,
too lofty for me to attain.

PSALM 139:6

I had it all figured out. Completely mapped. Couldn't be any more perfect. Surely, God would agree…wouldn't He? *Please?*

I'd been pursuing job prospects in Portland, Oregon, for several weeks and was growing desperate. Why did it seem so hard? What did these West Coast folks have against a Wisconsin boy? Never before had I encountered any trouble finding work, and now all I needed was a few hours each week to help get me through grad school. A few lousy hours! Was that too much to ask?

Apparently it was.

Days went by. Weeks passed. Nothing opened up. Three months went by, then four. Zilch.

Finally, one morning while scanning the classifieds, I saw it, shining out from the gray newsprint like a shaft of sun breaking through a heavy overcast. *Praise God!* The PR department of a local college needed a part-time writer for up to twenty hours a week. *Bingo!* How great was *that?* I held a bachelor's in journalism; I had worked as a reporter for two midwestern newspapers; and these new job hours fit my schedule to a T. *Lord,* I exulted, *this is PERfect! Oh, how could I ever have doubted You?*

Immediately I drafted a snappy letter of inquiry and zipped it off in the mail. It couldn't be long now!

It wasn't. Two weeks later I received a standardized rejection notice.

"Father," I complained, "what's going on here? This position was perfect! I needed that job! I've just about run through my savings, and if I don't find work soon, I'm going to have to move back home. Don't You *want* me to finish school?"

He didn't answer (at least, not so I could hear). So there I sat, stewing about my future. I'd told a few friends about my dilemma, but what help could they bring?

A few nights later I found out. My old Wisconsin buddy, Pat, worked with a large staff of volunteers in a church youth program. During an evening prayer session, he described to them how I'd have to pack up and leave if I didn't find work soon. Someone spoke up. "We're hiring at the publishing house," he said. "Why don't you have him give my boss a call?"

I did, and soon I found myself sitting across from the smiling face of Fae Brown. "It's telephone marketing," she was saying. "You'd be calling Christian bookstores across the country, selling them our books." I said I'd give it a try, though I had my doubts.

(A scene flooded my memory: One frigid Saturday afternoon many years before, dead of winter, dirty snow piled two feet deep. Three fellow newspaper boys and I are to canvass the neighborhood for new subscribers—something I loathe. When the others disperse in the gray coldness, I pick one old home, obviously vacant, and ring the doorbell. After no one answers, I skitter away and spend the next several hours aimlessly wandering back alleyways. "Nobody was interested," I say, quite truthfully, when I return to the warm truck.)

For a week and a half I trudged to work, shoulders stooped, feet dragging, the world's most reluctant telemarketer. I racked my brains for every excuse I could think of to avoid picking up that horrid phone and talking to a stranger. I despised it. *This is the worst job I've ever had,* I kept telling myself. Finally I could handle it no longer. For better or for worse, I decided to spill my guts. "Fae," I told my gracious boss, "this is the worst job I've ever had. I'm not doing you any good, and I'm not doing myself any good. So if there's someplace else in the company I can go, that would be great, but I CANNOT stay here."

Amazingly, the company "just happened" to have an opening in its warehouse, and for the next several months I shipped Christian books around the world. During that time I met a couple of the company's editors. Their job intrigued me. I wondered how I'd like that kind of work. Almost as an afterthought, I started praying about such a move, and one year later I joined the company as a full-time editor. Sixteen years afterward, I'm still writing and editing books—and I love it!

Now, what might have happened had God actually given me that college PR job? Where would I be now if He hadn't kept me from any job *at all* until that loathsome telemarketing position opened up? How would I have ended up where I am unless He first kept me around the warehouse long enough to get my foot in the door of the editorial department?

When I begin to ponder the infinite intelligence behind all of God's loving actions on my behalf, my mind simply locks up. I can't fathom it. How does He know exactly when and where to fit in each puzzle piece of my life? How can He foresee all the possible roadblocks and detours that I might drive into were it not for His kind intervention? How is He able to know which of my prayers to grant, which to deny, and how to encourage me when I think I'm being ignored? (I keep hearing the voice of Ruth Bell Graham, the wife of evangelist Billy Graham: "If God had answered every prayer of mine, I would have married the wrong man seven times.")

In the end, all I can do is gladly echo the words of David:

> *Such knowledge is too wonderful for me,*
> *too lofty for me to attain.*

All I can do is shout an amen as Isaiah speaks for God: "As the heavens are higher than the earth, so are my ways higher than your ways and my thoughts than your thoughts" (55:9).

All I can do is exult with the apostle Paul: "Oh, the depth of the riches of the wisdom and knowledge of God! How unsearchable his judgments, and his paths beyond tracing out!" (Romans 11:33).

What a Wonder!

What a wonder is our God! And what a never-ending wonder is His work on our behalf!

Yet how quickly we seem to forget those comforting thoughts. No matter how often we read of His lofty majesty—"How awesome is the LORD Most High, the great King over all the earth!" (Psalm 47:2)—we tend to forget His greatness when circumstances refuse to "heel" like a well-trained dog. Somehow it slips our mind that our God, who is "wonderful in counsel and magnificent in wisdom" (Isaiah 28:29), might actually have plans for us that far outstrip our ability to comprehend. So we fret and worry and stew and fuss over plans gone awry, never stopping to consider that, just maybe, the Lord's "knowledge is too wonderful for me, too lofty for me to attain."

Do me a favor, would you? The next time you're tempted to grow anxious about your life—when you're just sure that God couldn't possibly take you in a direction better than the one you had in mind—stop and consider my friend Slim. I'll let Slim introduce himself:

> Hi! I'm Slim, and I'm a cartoon character. I live on this crisp, white sheet of paper. I like it; it's home. Mountains, sunsets, animals, trees—all kinds of things seem to pop up around me at any time. And they can disappear almost as quickly as they show up too. Why? I don't know. The truth is, I don't know where they come from or where they go. Some strange cartoon character once tried to tell me something about an "artist," but I didn't

quite get it. You see, I'm not the metaphysical type. I'm a *realist.*

Yesterday I met another cartoon character—a weird, stick-legged kind of fellow who suddenly appeared right beside me. (Like I said, that's the way things work around here.) He started talking right away, filling up the page with his dialogue balloons. He told me that we live in a two-dimensional world. Well, *of course* we do. That's reality. There's height and there's width. That's it. That's the universe in a nutshell. How could there be any more?

Well, the stick-looking guy *(please,* tell me I don't look like *him!)* asked me if I could imagine *three* dimensions. "You would have length, breadth, and something called 'depth,'" he said. *Depth?* What's that? More metaphysical nonsense, if you ask me. He asked if I could imagine stepping "out" of the paper into a "three-dimensional" world. He told me that sometimes he feels a little skinny—that everything seems just "flat" to him. I told him he'd better stop that kind of talk right away. I've seen better looking characters than *him* get erased!

Anyway, how absurd to try thinking of life in three dimensions! I mean, what would you do with another dimension? I'm sure I can't imagine—and I really don't

like to think about it. No, what we have here is all there
is. If I'm sure about anything, I'm sure about *that*. (Have
I told you I'm a realist?)

Well, looks like the mountains are disappearing.
And—great staples! Is that a dinosaur forming over in
the left corner? I'd better check it out. 'Bye!

Now that you've met Slim, what do you think of his two-
dimensional mind passing judgment on our three-dimensional world?
Ridiculous, isn't it? Silly. Foolish. The height of ignorance, even.

And…maybe a little like you and me trying to imagine eternity?

The fact is, when you and I place our lives in the hands of the Creator of the Universe, we leave behind the limited realm of three
dimensions (plus one of time, if you prefer) and step into the limitless,
divine domain of infinity. From our vantage point, we can no more
figure out what God might be planning to do with our lives than Slim
can decipher what his artist might be up to.

Of course, there are important differences between Slim's perspective and our own. The most critical is that Slim doesn't know
his creator personally—remember, he considers the whole concept of
some all-powerful artist as little more than a myth, or a psychological
crutch for weak cartoon characters. The artist who gives him existence
(me) hasn't promised him life or beauty or love or joy or any of the
eye-popping gifts our God has sworn to us. Slim doesn't have any
promise remotely like this:

> You have made known to me the path of life;
>> you will fill me with joy in your presence,
>> with eternal pleasures at your right hand.
>> (Psalm 16:11)

Really, about the only thing Slim has in common with you and me is that he isn't equipped to understand (even dimly) anything outside of his limited framework.

But what if I were to give him such an understanding? What if I were to promise him that one day he could replace his gray flatness for the joys of depth? (It would give new meaning to a body *raised* to newness of life!) What if I could make him understand that, although he couldn't comprehend how I planned to do it, I would see him through safely to the end? Maybe then he'd write something like this: "He has made everything beautiful in its time. He has also set eternity in the hearts of men; yet they cannot fathom what God has done from beginning to end" (Ecclesiastes 3:11).

The Only Safe Route

When we turn our thoughts to the measureless wisdom of God, how can we fail to join our voices and exclaim with David, "Such knowledge is too wonderful for me, too lofty for me to attain"!

David marveled at the priceless treasures of divine insight that shone through the golden stones of heaven. The sight both drew and burned his spiritual eyes. In another place he would write, "My heart is not proud, O LORD, my eyes are not haughty; I do not concern myself with great matters or things too wonderful for me. But I have stilled and quieted my soul; like a weaned child with its mother, like a weaned child is my soul within me. O Israel, put your hope in the LORD both now and forevermore" (Psalm 131).

When we're finished thinking as deeply as we can, that's really the only safe route to take. God's thoughts tower over our own like the Eiffel Tower over a centipede, like Mount Everest over a mole, like the moon over a pebble sunk deep in the Mariana Trench.

When we catch ourselves murmuring about broken plans or unclear paths, we must learn to say to God, as did Job, "I know that you can do all things; no plan of yours can be thwarted.... Surely I spoke of things I did not understand, things too wonderful for me to know" (Job 42:2,3). And when our way grows hazy and the road ahead of us disappears in dense fog, we must train ourselves, like David, to "put our hope in the Lord both now and forevermore."

Slim can't do that, but you can. Slim can't escape from his two-dimensional, white-paper world. He'll never know anything but "the shallow end."

Not so you! The God and Father of our Lord Jesus Christ invites you to step into His universe and experience its limitless possibilities. No, you can't understand it. But that isn't the point. The point is *following*. And the depths of infinity promise a lot better swim than anything you can know on the surface!

—*S.H.*

4

global positioning

He is with me everywhere

Where can I go from your Spirit?

    Where can I flee from your presence?

If I go up to the heavens, you are there;

    if I make my bed in the depths, you are there.

If I rise on the wings of the dawn,

    if I settle on the far side of the sea,

even there your hand will guide me,

    your right hand will hold me fast.

PSALM 139:7-10

We rolled into Pittsburgh late at night. I had no idea how to reach Mars.

Henry, my Tanzanian traveling companion, kept urging the obvious. "Why don't you stop?" he groused. "Why don't you ask for directions? *Foolish* boy!"

Henry had become increasingly impatient as the evening wore on. Weariness and hunger will do that to you.

"I'm a little turned around," I shot back. "What am I supposed to say? 'Could you please tell me how to get to Mars?'"

Henry lapsed into Swahili, his habit whenever he became excited or upset. I really couldn't blame him. This distinguished, older African man had been compelled to ride across America with a directionally challenged kid in his early twenties. Our boss had mandated that I drive, which greatly offended Henry. He had further directed that I control the money (which I lost). *That* offended Henry even more. To top it off, our budget-minded company had guaranteed us a room at a Motel 6 in Mars, Pennsylvania. We simply had to find it. We had no money to stay anywhere else.

Finally, in desperation, I did ask for directions. Half a dozen times. But I could make sense of neither the contradictory instructions nor the clipped Pittsburgh accents. So on we drove, around and around the River City, over bridges, through tunnels, down mean back streets, and past dark neighborhoods. We cruised slowly through run-down areas of the city where unsavory characters sat smoking on the curbs. On one narrow street, a driverless car burst into flames on the curb just ahead of us.

Henry, chain-smoking Lucky Strikes and squinting to read the map under the dome light, would now and then shout directions.

"IST!"

"Ist?"

"*Foolish* boy! Go ist! You have been going west. Mars is *ist*."

I went ist. And south and north and to all points of the compass. But it was no good. I couldn't find Mars. I couldn't even get out of

Pittsburgh. I was as lost and forlorn as I had ever been in my short life.

He Is There

It's easy to get lost while trying to navigate an unfamiliar piece of real estate. No well-known landmarks. No recognizable features. Everything is totally new. The scenery might fairly burst with beauty, but if you don't know where you are, none of it brings much comfort.

Launching into a new phase of life is a lot like trying to find Mars. To this day, as I recall that humid summer night, my memories are creased with purgatory visions of interminable bridges, dark streets, and confusing road signs. And yet I understand that Pittsburgh perennially gets named one of America's most livable cities.

How I would have loved to employ Global Positioning System technology that awful night in 1976! With GPS, a man or woman's geographic position on the planet can be pinpointed to within a single yard. But back then, GPS didn't exist—at least not in a usable form.

It's too bad I didn't stop and recall the words of Psalm 139, where David offers some comforting counsel to those who long for direction on dark nights. Millennia before the advent of GPS, the young Israelite pondered a "system" that could trace an individual's precise location wherever he or she might wander on the face of the earth. David, however, wasn't talking about a space-based, radio-navigation system or twenty-four orbiting satellites beaming streams of information to ground stations. David needed only one Reference Point.

All he needed was God.

> *Where can I go from your Spirit?*
> > *Where can I flee from your presence?*
> *If I go up to the heavens, you are there;*
> > *if I make my bed in the depths, you are there.*
> *If I rise on the wings of the dawn,*
> > *if I settle on the far side of the sea,*
> *even there your hand will guide me,*
> > *your right hand will hold me fast.*

WHAT SPARKED THE PSALM?

When did David compose such words? He might have scratched them out as a teenager, late at night over the red embers of a dying fire. Wrapping his cloak tighter about his young shoulders, he might have looked up into the vault of heaven and sensed…the Presence.

But why? Why should God know or care about the location of a simple shepherd boy? Why should it concern the mighty Lord of the universe whether David warmed himself by a fire of sticks, knelt by a spring to drink, scaled a windswept hill, or reclined in the shadow of a towering rock on a long afternoon? Who was David? Nobody. A tiny fleck of human flesh in a vast cosmos, with neither prominence nor prospects. He was accounted the least in his large family. So who was he to gain the notice of the Creator? As he would say to the Lord in later years, "Who am I, O Sovereign LORD, and what is my family, that you have brought me this far?" (2 Samuel 7:18). It just didn't add up.

And yet, sitting by his little fire, young David felt wrapped in divine presence. God was there! And God knew *David* was there, too. The shepherd boy took comfort that the God of heaven had noted and marked his precise position. Just as He does yours, right now.

Or maybe David penned this psalm some years later when he slew the Philistine champion Goliath. By this act he achieved instant celebrity; the king and the military elite took notice. Prince Jonathan pledged lasting friendship. Women in the streets sang ballads about the ruddy young warrior who dispatched the Philistines and saved Israel's honor.

But almost as quickly as he acquired fame, David was branded a traitor by a jealous king and became a fugitive, running for his life. Hounded into the wilderness by pursuing soldiers, he hid in desolate lands, sometimes taking shelter in a honeycomb of limestone caves.

Might David have composed his psalm as he sat in the mouth of such a cave at twilight, looking out across a dry waste, listening to the sigh of wind over lonely lands and ragged shoulders of stone? He felt so tiny. So insignificant. So alone. In one chance encounter with Saul, he protested, "The king of Israel has come out to look for a flea—as one hunts a partridge in the mountains" (1 Samuel 26:20).

Why pursue me? he wondered. *Why stalk me day and night from one end of the land to the other? Who am I, anyway? A tiny flea crawling across a mountain slope. A solitary bird roosting in a trackless forest. A bit of fallen leaf flying in the wind. Who would bother to trace such an insignificant thing across the land?*

Yet even as David breathed the question, he already knew the answer. Saul would do so because of his hatred. And the Spirit of God would do so because of His love.

AN AWESOME THOUGHT

David might flee the king's army, dodge the assassins, and slip around Saul's hit squads and bullyboys. But he could not flee the presence of God. It went with him like his own thoughts, like the throb of blood in his temples or the surge of air in his lungs. He might hide in the land of the Philistines or take refuge with the king of Gath. He might buy passage on a merchant ship and sail to the edge of the known world. Yet the moment he stepped down the gangway, God would be there to greet him.

Have you stopped to think about that? Where David went, God went. David could walk away from his father, his brothers, his friends, and his fellow soldiers, but he could never walk away from his Lord. And the realization gripped him with awe.

Does this staggering thought strike you with equal force? Does the idea that God walks with you wherever you roam fill you with astonished gratitude? It's meant to. Like David, you might feel as though you're rocketing into dangerous, uncharted heavens. *But God is there, waiting for you.* Or perhaps it feels as though you're about to make your bed in the black depths, impossibly far from all you've ever known. *But God is there, watching over you.* Or maybe you are literally about to board an early morning international flight for a new life on the far side of the sea. *But even so far away, God is there, welcoming you into His presence.*

GPS might be wonderful, but it can never compare to God! David marveled at a God who could never lose sight of him even for an instant—in the heights or depths, in the mountains or on the sea, in time and beyond time. Earth-orbiting GPS satellites could never track him (or you) on the dark side of the moon or on the southern polar cap of Mars or to the nameless desolation of a planet orbiting Alpha Centauri.

But God could.

The two dozen satellites of the GPS system might trail a living human being across the skin of our globe. But they are powerless to follow a soul into eternity.

God can go where we never could. God can speak where all of man's wondrous technology is as useless as two tin cans connected by a string. God can follow you from life into death and on into eternity. God can track you no matter what occurs in your life, no matter where you go or what you do. He can walk into your dreams. He can penetrate your fears. He can reach through your confusion. He can speak to your spirit even when your body can't respond. He can lay His finger on your heart when others might shrug their shoulders and walk away. God can touch your heart just as surely as He did the "valiant men" of 1 Samuel 10:26. As one author has written about this passage:

> The touch of God on one's heart is an awesome thing. It is awesome because the heart is so precious to us—so deep and intimate and personal. When the heart is touched, we are deeply touched. Someone has gotten through protective layers to the center. We have been known. We have been uncovered and seen.
>
> The touch of God is an awesome thing because God is God. Just think of what is being said here! God touched them. Not a wife. Not a child. Not a parent. Not a counselor. But God. The One with infinite power in the universe. The One with infinite authority, infinite wisdom, infinite love, infinite goodness, infinite purity, and infinite justice. That One touched their hearts. How does the circumference of Jupiter touch the edge of a molecule, let alone penetrate to its nucleus?
>
> The touch of God is awesome because it is a touch. It is a real connection. That it involves the heart is awesome. That it involves God is awesome.... The valiant men were not just spoken to. They were not just swayed by a divine influence. They were not just seen and known from outside. God, with infinite condescension,

touched their hearts. God was that close. And they were not consumed.[1]

What worries you most, right now? What causes you the most anxiety? Whatever it is, take great courage in this: God will go with you wherever your feet may wander. Eons ago the patriarch Job made that crucial discovery. He learned that God enters into the springs of the sea, walks the recesses of the deep, and peers through the gates of deep darkness (Job 38:16-17). God enters into the storehouses of the snow and hail, guides constellations with His hand, soars with the hawk, and nests with the eagle (38:22; 38:31-32; 39:26-27).

And He knows where you are. Right now. Wherever you go through the years of life, He will go with you. His eye sees you. His mind ponders your steps. His heart yearns for you. His hand reaches for yours and will guide your way. In solemn truth, you will *never* be alone.

Not even for a heartbeat.

Not even in Pittsburgh.

—*L.L.*

---

1. John Piper, *A Godward Life* (Sisters, Oreg.: Multnomah Publishers, 1997), 79-80.

a hand in the dark

He guides me and holds me close

Your hand will guide me,
your right hand will hold me fast.

PSALM 139:10

Have you ever prayed for specific guidance about a situation or decision—and then felt disappointed because the way still didn't seem clear?

You pray for the fog to lift...but a heavy bank of it clings for days—dense, wet, and cold.

You pray for the darkness to roll back...but you still can't see your hand in front of your face.

You pray for precise directions...yet the days go by and no map floats down from the blue sky or arrives at your door by Angelic Parcel Service.

Why doesn't God come through for you? Why doesn't He show the way? Why does He hold back vital information? Doesn't He care about what you're enduring?

It may be that God has a different idea about your needs than you do. What you *want* is road map…but what you really *need* is a Guide.

The Atlas Junkie

I've always been something of a map addict. I applaud when someone draws a simple, precise map to a destination instead of rattling off a batch of verbal directions, adding that inevitable postscript, "You can't miss it!"

Wanna bet? You have no idea how many times I've "missed it." On rare occasions (and forced by bitter necessity) I will roll down the window of my car and ask some stranger for directions. But it's all for naught. Before the power window rolls back to the top, I've forgotten everything. It's a blank slate.

So please don't *tell* me where to drive. Draw me a map! Pencil in a few landmarks. And don't forget to include north, south, east, and west.

For Christmas one year I received an atlas of topographical maps for every inch of the state of Oregon. Oh, glorious! On *those* maps, I can identify swamps, waterfalls, dunes, dams, caves, mines, lava flows, and glaciers—just in case I encounter something on the way to the store. I can track rising and falling elevation, foot by foot. By poring over my "topo" maps last year, I was able to identify, locate, and experience two of central Oregon's most unheralded natural wonders. Who needs Mount Rushmore or the Grand Canyon when you've got Crack-in-the-Ground and Hole-in-the-Ground?

I like to know where I've been, where I am, and what awaits me on the road ahead. I don't like unpleasant surprises. I don't like detours. And I loathe being lost. So just hand me a map, give me a minute or two to get oriented, and I'll be okay.

That's why it's been such a struggle through my life to pray for guidance and wisdom. What I really want from God (and it seems like He ought to realize it by now) is a road map. It doesn't have to be elaborate or fancy—just a diagram of the next few months scribbled out on the back of an envelope. Let me spread the thing out on the kitchen table or the living room floor and get the full picture. I want to know how high I'll have to climb, how low I'll have to descend, how long the desert will last, and how many rest areas I'll find in between. Doesn't that sound reasonable?

But God never works that way. He never sends me a map. He never faxes me an itinerary. He never tells me what's around the bend in the road or what I can expect on tomorrow's leg of the journey.

All He ever does is offer to come along as a Guide.

GOD AT MY SIDE

For David, the offer of a Guide seemed to be enough—and a vast comfort to his heart. In Psalm 139 he wrote:

> *Your hand will guide me,*
> *your right hand will hold me fast.*

In another psalm he made an even more amazing declaration: "Even when walking through the dark valley of death I will not be afraid, for you are close beside me, guarding, guiding all the way" (Psalm 23:4, TLB).

David, David—how can you speak that way? The valley is shadowed and dark. You can't see more than a foot in front of your feet. It's a road that bristles with danger and deadly peril. You've never been that way before, and you have no map. How can you *not* be afraid?

And David replies, "I don't have to see the road ahead. I don't have to know where I've been, where I am, or where I'm going. The only thing that matters is Who I'm *with*. If God is at my side, I'll be okay—no matter what."

And so it has been through the years. God does not offer maps, flight plans, or extended itineraries to His earthbound children. Yet He continually offers Himself as Guide. He will shepherd us through dark and rain and fog—and through bright sunlit days—with a hand on our shoulder.

When a small band of Jewish exiles set out on the long journey from Persia to the ruins of Jerusalem, it was a scary proposition. No one had returned to the old country in a generation. Hostile adversaries and unknown perils might lurk over the horizon. Yet Ezra the priest sensed that "the hand of our God was on us, and he protected us from enemies and bandits along the way" (Ezra 8:31).

In a season of great national upheaval and vast dangers, the Lord whispered in Judah's ears,

Do not fear, for I am with you;
>   do not be dismayed, for I am your God.
I will strengthen you and help you;
>   I will uphold you with my righteous right hand....
For I am the LORD, your God,
>   who takes hold of your right hand
and says to you, Do not fear;
>   I will help you. (Isaiah 41:10,13)

In a time of confusion and sorrow, the disciple Thomas wanted a road map to the Father's house in heaven. Jesus had just told His little band that He was going away to a place they could not immediately reach. "In my Father's house," He told them, "are many rooms; if it were not so, I would have told you. I am going there to prepare a place for you.... You know the way to the place where I am going" (John 14:2,4).

Thomas didn't get it. How could they possibly know the way to "the Father's house"? Where were the instructions? Where were the travel brochures? *Where was the map?*

"Lord," he protested, "we don't know where you are going, so how can we know the way?" (14:5).

At that point, I believe, the Son of God looked His dear friend square in the eyes and replied, "I am the way and the truth and the life. No one comes to the Father except through me" (14:6).

In other words, *You don't need a map, Thomas. You need a Guide. I am the Guide. I am the way to eternal life. Abide in Me!*

In our distress and anxiety, we often demand from the Lord detailed, specific answers—answers we presume will relieve our stress, calm our spirits, and quiet our churning thoughts. We say to ourselves, *If He would only tell me this or that by tomorrow, I would have peace.* Yet the truth is, if we had the immediate answers to "this" or "that," there would be even more puzzles on our doorstep the next morning.

We don't need "answers," we need Jesus.

We don't need details, we need a Guide.

We don't need an itinerary, we need His steady hand on our shoulders, leading us through the perilous terrain of a fallen world under enemy control.

PERILS UNSEEN

Bob, my father-in-law, hunts deer every fall in the mountains of north-central California. A number of farmers and ranchers in the area are willing to let individuals or small groups hunt on their property, if the hunters ask permission and show respect for the land. My father-in-law is one of the most congenial men I've ever met. It would take a surpassingly cranky landowner to turn him down.

Last year he approached a rancher to ask if he might drive through a certain gate to do some hunting in the evening. When shadows lengthen and the October sun slips low in the west, deer begin to venture forth from their hiding places to graze.

The rancher gave Bob a thoughtful look and said, "Yeah, you can come on the land. But you'd better let me ride with you in the truck for awhile. Want to show you some things."

Now, I can imagine most men thinking, *Oh, come on! SHOW me some things? Why do I need a passenger? Either let me in or tell me to stay out. I know how to drive, and I know how to hunt. I'm a big boy, and I don't need a chaperone!*

Bob, however, being the man he is, cheerfully assented, and the pair drove through the gate onto the ranch. They had been skimming across a wide, seemingly featureless field when the rancher suddenly said, "You'd better start slowing down."

Why? Had he seen a deer? Bob pulled his foot off the accelerator. But why stop? As far as he could see, there were no creeks, gullies, or fences. Just a wide pasture stretching out to the dusky foothills.

"Okay," said the rancher. "You'd better park right here. Want to show you something."

Bob did as he was told. They got out of the truck in the cool, mountain air and began walking. Then the rancher put his hand on Bob's shoulder and said, "Look up ahead."

My father-in-law walked slowly forward and then stopped dead in his tracks. Cleaving at right angles across their path—and across the pasture as far as he could see in both directions—was a yawning, black tear in the surface of the earth. Where they stood, the crack was probably thirty feet across. Peering over the edge, the hair on Bob's neck bristled.

Where was the bottom?

The sheer, rock-ribbed sides of the great volcanic fissure plunged to unknown depths. Cold, still air seemed to exhale from the blackness below.

The rancher pointed. "Look, see down on those rocks?"

Bob squinted his eyes and thought he saw a couple of birds.

"Owls," said the rancher. "They like nesting in there 'cause it's always night."

Walking back to the truck, Bob marveled at how difficult it was to see the fissure from just yards away. A man on a fast-running horse could simply disappear and never be seen again. And the abyss was certainly wide enough to swallow a pickup truck.

Bob smiled to himself. Having a guide wasn't such a bad thing! He gained a new appreciation for a man who knew the terrain—and where to park the truck.

He Knows the Way

What would I really *do* if God gave me a "map" of the year ahead, showing me every bend in the road? Knowing my own stubborn self, I would probably say, "Thank You very much, Lord. This will do nicely. I'll be fine on my own, now. Check in with You next year." And I would walk away from Him, depending on my own ability to find my own way and meet my own needs.

How foolish. I am not "fine on my own." I'm a *disaster* on my own. I fall into Satan's traps. I blunder over cliffs. I entangle myself in webs of deceit. I wander into swamps of lust, anger, greed, and pride.

In a sense, I already have a wonderful "map." It's a beautiful piece of work, thousands of years old, printed on India paper and encased between two covers of top grain cowhide.

It's called a Bible.

Yet apart from the daily guidance of God's Holy Spirit, I can't even follow *that* set of instructions.

Do you know what I need? I need a hand on my shoulder. I need an alert eye and an iron grip to pull me back from the precipice. I need a voice whispering words of warning and encouragement in my ear. I need Someone who has walked the paths ahead of me and knows the way.

So do you, my friend. The way ahead is too perilous to count on dead reckoning. The road before you offers too many vistas and wonders for you to let yourself become bogged down on a bad road through the swamps.

No atlas of human wisdom can lift you out of knee-deep mud. That takes a ready hand and a surpassingly strong arm. A map, after all, simply tells you where people have been over a thousand yesterdays. Jesus is the only Guide who knows your tomorrows.

—L.L.

a sure and steady light

He shines His light on times of confusion

If I say, "Surely the darkness will hide me
and the light become night around me,"
even the darkness will not be dark to you;
the night will shine like the day,
for darkness is as light to you.

PSALM 139:11-12

Do you like the dark? I don't mean, can you tolerate it or are you able to control your fear of it. I mean, do you *like* the dark, do you *enjoy* it, would you *choose* to live in a world where total darkness reigned?

The late science fiction writer Isaac Asimov was only twenty-one years old when he published his famous short story *Nightfall*, about a planet illuminated by six suns. The inhabitants of Lagash knew nothing but constant day; to experience darkness they had to visit a cave, and who was crazy enough to do that? One amusement park opened an attraction called the "Tunnel of Mystery," in which patrons rode for fifteen terrifying minutes through a pitch-black, mile-long under-ground passage. Authorities quickly shut down the ride when an alarming percentage of thrill-seekers went mad.

The bulk of *Nightfall* describes what happens when scientists conclude that every 2,049 years a mysterious orbiting body shrouds Lagash in the deepest night, revealing a host of previously hidden stars and precipitating a planetwide social meltdown that always results in a new Stone Age.

I remember the first time I read Asimov's remarkable story. I couldn't help but put myself in the characters' place. *Would I go mad in the "Tunnel of Mystery"? If all the light of the world suddenly went out, how would I react? Would I, too, take to burning everything in sight to help relieve the thick darkness?*

I think *Nightfall* works on several levels, not the least of which is the psychological. As one of the story's characters explains, we are "born with three instinctive fears: of loud noises, of falling, and of the absence of light."[1] We don't especially like the dark, unless we're try-ing to sleep (and even then some of us have night-lights). It scares us. Who knows what might be lurking in the blackness?

When I was a little boy growing up in Beloit, Wisconsin, my mother used to dry damp shirts and blouses by hanging them from bedroom doorframes. This was fine during daylight hours, but some-how, after dark...*they stirred to life.* I often awoke in the middle of the

---

1. Isaac Asimov, *Nightfall and Other Stories* (New York: Del Ray, 1969), 22.

night, groggy and disoriented, and caught a quick glimpse—quick because I'd immediately duck under the covers—of squadrons of these silent, ghostly monsters levitating in the darkness. I wanted to run, but how could I? *They were blockading my doorway!*

Now understand, I wasn't especially afraid of the dark. Most of the time the gloom didn't bother me at all. Yet every once in awhile it had a way of scaring the bejabbers out of me.

Have you ever known that kind of fear—the raw, churning panic that tears at your gut when some hidden enemy blows out all the lights? King David did. In Psalm 143:3-4 he wrote, "The enemy pursues me, he crushes me to the ground; he makes me dwell in darkness like those long dead. So my spirit grows faint within me; my heart within me is dismayed."

Groping about in the dark can make any of us feel afraid and faint. We're built for the light, not the gloom. And yet we live in a world that spends half of every day in darkness. Some of that blackest night is bound to spill over into our lives.

And unfortunately it doesn't stop there. Whenever we launch out into some new venture or phase of life, the sky can often look more black than bright. Unfamiliar surroundings cast strange and threatening shadows. We can't quite tell what looms ahead. *Are those shirts drying in the doorframes, or...?*

David knew such unsettling times very well, but he also knew where to direct his frightened heart when he felt it trembling in his chest. He declared to God,

If I say, "Surely the darkness will hide me
and the light become night around me,"
even the darkness will not be dark to you;
the night will shine like the day,
for darkness is as light to you.

Talk about taking the fear out of the dark! David might not be able to see his way through the thick blackness, but it posed no problem for God. Even a cat needs *some* light to see, but David's Lord needed no light at all. Dark, light; gloom, brilliance; night, day—it's all the same to God. He sees no better (or worse) in one condition than in the other. He sees it all. Everywhere. All the time.

Including you.

A "DARK NIGHT OF THE SOUL"

Let's be clear. David isn't speaking of literal light and darkness in this passage. He's describing in a poetic way the hardships and difficulties of life that occasionally try to swallow us whole. He's using the metaphor of darkness to picture how his heart recoils in anxiety and fear when his well-laid plans crumble and his enemies rise up with murder in their throats.

Have you ever felt like that? Have you ever looked forward to some exciting possibility or long-awaited event, only to see it snatched away at the last moment? It's as if all your hopes and dreams sink into the darkest reaches of a menacing black mist.

I felt just like that toward the end of my second year of seminary. I know now that a frantic schedule, coupled with a growing dissatisfaction with my school's theological direction, stoked the furnace of stress in my body to temperatures far beyond what it could handle. By the spring of 1982 I had developed an ulcer (although I didn't yet know it), couldn't sleep, and began to imagine I was dying.

It was awful. I couldn't stop obsessing about my health. I thought about it in class. I thought about it at dinner. I thought about it in bed. I monitored every little pain, noted every twitch. I began taking long walks around the campus—always at night—trying to pray, but usually ending up focusing on my physical troubles. Often I wound up in the library, poring over a massive medical textbook to see if I could identify my mysterious (and, I was convinced, deadly) malady.

I visited the school nurse. I spoke with a doctor on the phone. And finally I packed up and left school, just a couple of weeks shy of the end of the semester. I drove the six-hour trip to my parents' home, noting along the way (in my rearview mirror) that my tongue looked, well, odd. *Did it always have that strange coating?*

Things went on like that for the next six months. I retreated deeper and deeper into myself, ever more convinced that I didn't have long to live—despite what the doctor said. At the lowest point of my descent, in the middle of an autumn afternoon, I lay sprawled across my unmade bed, boiling with anger.

How could God have allowed this? I never rebelled against Him. I never fell into the kinds of sin that tripped up so many of my friends. I've served God my whole life. I even went to seminary to learn how to serve Him better. And this is how He repays me? By killing me?

I was just getting started.

Maybe I don't really know Him at all. Maybe He's nothing like what the Bible says He is. I don't doubt that He's all-powerful, but what if He's not all-loving, as the Bible claims? What if He gets His kicks by dangling a few promises out there until someone takes Him up on one, then laughs and laughs when He pulls the rug out from under the poor fool? What if He's really an all-powerful devil?

You can't go very far down that pitch-black road before you're forced to make a series of critical choices:

- Is God a liar, or not?
- Is the Word of God true or false?
- Did Jesus Christ rise from the dead, or did He stay in the tomb?

In quick succession a further set of tough questions bombarded my reeling mind:

- What caused the apostle Paul's conversion, if not a risen Lord?
- How could the Jewish race still exist, if a promise-keeping God hadn't sustained them?
- How could so many Bible prophecies have been fulfilled, if an eternally loving God hadn't inspired them?

By the end of that afternoon I had begun my long climb out of the darkness. Don't misunderstand—I didn't leap from that bed a "cured man." But as dusk settled in and the shadows lengthened, I also noticed thin rays of sunlight streaming through the windows. From that day on my "dark night of the soul" (a phrase coined by sixteenth century Spanish mystic Saint John of the Cross) began to abate. I took the first step on my journey back into the light.

And do you know what I found? I discovered that God—the God David knew so well—had been with me all along. He hadn't abandoned me. He hadn't given up on me. He hadn't enjoyed my spiritual turmoil, but neither had He been swallowed up in the darkness that so tormented me. During the worst of those six months I truly felt lost in the dark, my very light remade into blackest night—and yet God, "who lives in unapproachable light" (1 Timothy 6:16), never once dropped me from His loving gaze. He never lost sight of me. He never grew confused. He never wondered for an instant how it all might turn out. Why not? Because the Bible is wonderfully true when it proclaims, "even the darkness will not be dark to you; the night will shine like the day, for darkness is as light to you."

Although I never want to endure such a time again, I must say that my confidence and trust in God and in His Son Jesus Christ grew more during my "dark night of the soul" than during any sunnier period of life. Spiritual photosynthesis, it seems, can operate in the dark as well as in the light.

I came to believe, to a far deeper degree than ever before, that my God delights in fulfilling the word He spoke through Isaiah the prophet:

> I will lead the blind by ways they have not known,
>   along unfamiliar paths I will guide them;

I will turn the darkness into light before them
>   and make the rough places smooth.
These are the things I will do;
>   I will not forsake them. (Isaiah 42:16)

ALL THE DIFFERENCE IN THE WORLD

It makes all the difference in the world if you truly believe that you serve a living God who reigns in unapproachable light, who longs to dispel your darkness and who remains eternally clear-eyed and forever watchful over every minute detail in every nook and cranny of your life.

Do *you* believe this? Do *you* know God as the one to whom the night shines like the day? Do *you* worship the God of Isaiah?

The sun will no more be your light by day,
>   nor will the brightness of the moon shine on you,
for the LORD will be your everlasting light,
>   and your God will be your glory. (Isaiah 60:19)

Do you exult in the God of Paul?

For God, who said, "Let light shine out of darkness,"
made his light shine in our hearts to give us the light of
the knowledge of the glory of God in the face of Christ.
(2 Corinthians 4:6)

Do you glory in the God of John?

This is the message we have heard from him and declare
to you: God is light; in him there is no darkness at all.
(1 John 1:5)

Several years ago I wrote a little book titled *No Night Too Dark:
How God Turns Defeat into Glorious Triumph*. In it I tried to show
through both Scripture and life examples how God delights in taking
the worst Satan can throw at us and transforming it into a trophy of
grace for His glory and our benefit. If anything, I believe more deeply
in that message today than when I wrote,

> When our world is caving in, when things look as grim
> as they possibly can, when it seems as though Satan has
> applied the *coup de grace* to our fondest hopes and
> greatest desires—at precisely that point the Strong One
> steps in and brandishes the very evil for His glory.
>
> This suggests even more than the glorious words of
> Romans 8:28: "And we know that in all things God
> works for the good of those who love him, who have
> been called according to his purpose." That wonderful
> text reminds us that God will use all of the events of our
> lives for our ultimate good. But God often goes beyond
> merely bringing good out of evil; frequently He uses *the
> very evil itself* to bless His people and bring glory to
> Himself.
>
> The God I know and love and serve not only makes
> all things work together for the good of those who love

Him, but sometimes He takes the very evil intended to destroy us and stands it on its head, so that even the evil itself works for our benefit and His glory.

Now, *that* is a God to worship! *That* is a God to adore!

And that is the God who fills the universe with His splendor—not some shuffling, half-dead, powerless deity who's in it way over his head.

So let me ask once more: what kind of God do *you* believe in? When the darkness closes in, does your god lose his vision? Does he grope about in the dark, mystified about the location or condition of his followers?

Or do you believe in the living God, the Holy One of Israel, to whom the night is as day and the deepest blackness as the light of a billion exploding suns? For if *this* God is *your* God, then no matter where your path takes you and no matter how dark the skies may grow, you will always be standing at the very center of His white-hot love and concern. And He knows how to take care of those who have captured His heart!

For the eyes of the LORD range throughout the earth to strengthen those whose hearts are fully committed to him. (2 Chronicles 16:9)

—*S.H.*

manufacturer's guarantee

He made me the way I am

For you created my inmost being;
>   you knit me together in my mother's womb.
I praise you because I am fearfully and wonderfully made;
>   your works are wonderful,
>   I know that full well.
My frame was not hidden from you
>   when I was made in the secret place.
When I was woven together in the depths of the earth,
>   your eyes saw my unformed body.

PSALM 139:13-16

Did you ever play the "what if" game?

Sometimes, to tease my teenagers, I will say to my wife (in their hearing), "Gosh, Babe, do you realize that if you had gone to the snack bar for a Coke instead of walking over to the meeting hall with your friends that day at summer camp back in '76, I might never have met you?" And then I will glance meaningfully at the kids, as if to say, "And you two wouldn't even exist."

They really hate that kind of talk. I do it to get a rise out of them, and (to my satisfaction) it always works. It gives you a queasy sense of vertigo to imagine your very existence might hang on such feeble threads of circumstance. It sends a little shiver down your spine to contemplate that, except for the merest whim or off chance, *you might never have come to be.*

If my kids knew the facts, they could do the same thing to me. What if my dad hadn't escaped that sinking aircraft carrier in World War II? What if he had decided to stay on the ranch in Nebraska instead of joining the Civilian Conservation Corps and coming out to Oregon (where he met Mom)? What if Dad and Mom had decided that two boys were already quite a handful, thank you, and they didn't need a third (me)?

What makes it all seem so appalling and lonely is to realize that you wouldn't even be missed if you were never born, because there never would have been a "you" at all.

Those thoughts used to bother me. They don't anymore. Do you know why? Because I know that I was on God's drawing board from all eternity. My existence has *never* hung by a thread of chance. In fact, "chance" has nothing to do with it. Before stars were flung into the void, before angel hosts watched the Creator form a universe out of nothing, before our own dappled blue planet was set spinning on its axis, I was in the mind of our eternal God.

And so were you.

It's true! Before the Wright Brothers soared at Kitty Hawk… before Napoleon staggered at Waterloo…before Columbus hoisted anchor…before Marco Polo strode into Cathay…before the Vandals rearranged Rome…before Moses stared in wonder at the burning bush…before Adam took his first joyous step on a new planet just out of the packing crate…God knew that you were to be.

Yes, you. Just as you are, right now.

Your vital statistics were on file before Eve gave birth to her first child. God knew who you were and where and when you would be born.

He knew your gender.

He knew your eye color.

He knew your birthmarks.

He knew your aversion to broccoli.

He knew your gifting and your potential.

He knew how many hairs would sprout on your head.

How could it be otherwise? If the eternal God does not have total knowledge of past, present, and future, He would no longer be God. There is no fact in the universe that God does not know. If you are reading these words, you *are* such a fact—and He has pondered your existence deep in the counsels of eternity.

The prophet Jeremiah had a bit of trouble with that concept. When "the word of the Lord" came to him as a young man, whispering that he was to be a mighty prophet of Yahweh, the thought staggered him.

Who was he to be a spokesman for God? He wouldn't even make it with the Jerusalem Toastmasters! Besides his painful lack of speaking abilities, he was young and inexperienced. How could he stand before kings and royal officials and proclaim God's messages of warning and doom? Could it be that the Lord had the wrong man?

Not a chance.

Listen to God's amazing words to His reluctant servant:

> Before I formed you in the womb I knew you,
> before you were born I set you apart;
> I appointed you as a prophet to the nations.
>   (Jeremiah 1:4-5)

Jeremiah had a high destiny before he was conceived.

So do you.

You Are No Accident

Such truths, however, don't capture a lot of airtime in today's world. Our secular culture—above all wanting to escape any accountability to a personal, holy God—has sold itself on a universe of blind, random chance.

This view insists that life—existence itself—is just a freak confluence of impersonal, natural forces. And if the cosmos itself is a colossal happenstance, a "big bang" in a nameless void, how much less worthy of notice is a single human life? It was only chance (they say) that put your parents together. Your conception was nothing more than an accident of fate. The fact that a particular sperm cell (out of millions) united with a particular microscopic egg amounts to nothing more than a roll of the cosmic dice. In other words, you're lucky to be alive (but don't place much significance on that fact). You are a chance built on chance a million times over—a fragile house of randomly drawn cards, dating back to that incomprehensible moment when "nothing" somehow gave birth to "everything."

Have you ever heard something like this? It wouldn't surprise me if someone told you that your birth was a "mistake." That you weren't even *wanted*. That your appearance in the world resulted from the failure of a normally reliable birth control method or a romantic tryst that got out of hand. If things had gone "according to plan," you wouldn't even be here.

I recently read about a teenage boy in our area who must have swallowed that line. He put a gun to his head and pulled the trigger because he accidentally put a dent in his dad's prized pickup. This boy apparently didn't consider his life as valuable as a fender on a Ford.

David would have none of that. The son of Jesse consigned such nihilistic nonsense back to the sewer out of which it crept. He would have labeled it for what it was (and is): a naked slander on the name of the living God.

Planned in Heaven

Your birth—an accident? An aimless, indiscriminate occurrence? Not on your life!

You made all the delicate, inner parts of my body,
David sang with wonder,
    and knit them together in my mother's womb....
You saw me before I was born
    and scheduled each day of my life
    before I began to breathe. (TLB)

Your parents may not have planned you, expected you, anticipated you, prepared for you, or even *desired* you. Your father may have split the scene before you were born, or your mother may have given you up for adoption. None of those things impact your value. Why not? Because you appeared on heaven's drawing board endless eons before you went into production on planet earth.

Your conception may have surprised your parents, but it was no surprise to heaven. You arrived precisely on schedule, exactly as it was planned before God said, "Let there be light."

He chose the time of your birth, the place of your birth, and the circumstances of your birth. He watched over your formation in the womb ("your eyes saw my unformed body") and carefully wired in the package of unique features that set you apart from every human being who ever lived or will live.

A Reason to Be

There is a reason you exist. God made only one of you, and He will never make another. You have a purpose to fulfill that no one else could ever accomplish in the same way. You have no need to compare yourself to others. Your strengths and weaknesses, your abilities and lack of abilities, fit into God's purposes and work together for His glory.

Perhaps, like me, you have wasted a lot of time wishing you could change certain fixed things about yourself. You want to look like him (or her) instead of you. You want to be able to do what he can do, or what she's so good at, instead of what God has enabled you to be and do.

I have fervently wished I had just a few basic handyman skills. Dads and husbands are supposed to be good at that stuff. But I have yet to find a left-handed hammer or screwdriver that fits my grip.

I wish I were a good conversationalist.

I wish I were two inches taller.

I wish I had a different profile.

Most of all, I wish I could be an impressive speaker. For years I've considered the crown of all talents to be the ability to stand before an audience and move its members with passion and wisdom and logic.

I don't have it. I can't do it. I've tried—again and again—but it just doesn't fly.

In my senior year of high school, I wrote a letter to my school paper: a brief, scathing denunciation of antiwar activities taking place in my liberal, university town. One of my older brothers fought on the front lines in Vietnam that year, and my heart moved me to support him as he had so often stuck up for me. My letter—a sharply honed arrow with a lethal, poisoned tip—hit precisely the target I had sighted in.

What a stir it created! It angered many of my dovish friends and came to the attention of the faculty. I was asked to appear before a senior humanities class to debate and defend my position.

I should have declined. I should have let the letter say it all. While my words on paper seemed sharp, cutting, and concise, my words before my classmates came out rambling, illogical, and choked with emotion—the difference between a razor-edged stiletto and a fat-handled butter knife. At the very moment when I needed cold logic, a calm countenance, and a coolly reasoned reply, my voice cracked, my lip trembled, and my hands shook.

And the competition blew me out of the room.

The antiwar forces at North Eugene High School rejoiced as the kid behind the potent letter turned out to be a paper tiger who couldn't begin to defend his position. What a humiliation! Bitterness over my failure consumed me. Why had God deprived me of the very gift I so needed and desired?

It wasn't until many years later that I began to appreciate the reach and power of the written word. Maybe it was the letter from Philadelphia that began to change my mind. A grateful father had taken the time to jot me a note. His twenty-two year old, mentally handicapped daughter had grown inconsolable following the death of her mother. No one could reach her. No one could comfort her or bring her out of her grief. And yet God in His sovereignty chose to use something I had written years earlier about heaven, in a children's book. When this dear young woman heard the words of that little book, she found immediate comfort and relief—not in my words but in the truth of

God's Word made clear. She finally understood that she would see her mom again and that somehow it was going to be all right. God's ability to use those few simple words to help one of His choice daughters awed me.

Some time later I received a request to reprint one of my magazine articles. The letter was postmarked, *The Outer Hebrides.* An Anglican pastor on a windswept island northwest of Scotland asked if he might use the article in his church newsletter. I stared at the envelope in wonder. And I asked myself, *When, in a hundred years of making speeches, might I have the opportunity to deliver words of encouragement to a group of believers on a tiny island in the North Sea?*

God has slowly begun to convince me how foolish it is to compare myself—my gifts, my opportunities, my open doors—with others. When He formed me in the womb, He already knew about a grieving young woman in Philadelphia who yearned for comfort in the darkest season of her life. Before I was ever conceived, His eyes saw a little congregation on the Isle of Lewis who needed a special word of grace in a wet, gray November.

He *used* me.

The wonder of it! It may not have been in the way I always wanted to be used or expected to be used, and yet the sovereign God of the universe wrote me into His eternal plan and chose to touch a few other lives through me. Awesome privilege!

May I ask you a question? Could it be that you haven't seen Him work through your life in the way you wished and hoped He would? Might you be a little disappointed that He hasn't given you *that* gift or *this* ability or *the other* opportunity, as He has one of your friends? Listen, the One who planned your arrival before He formed the angels knows how to use your unique gifting and circumstances to bring glory to His name. He will do it while you walk this earth—and He will continue to do it when you step out of this life into the life that never ends.

EVERYONE IS NECESSARY

I appreciate the reminder that Joni Eareckson Tada mined from the works of Charles H. Spurgeon. That grand old nineteenth-century pastor once suggested that the reason redeemed people will number more than the grains of sand on the beach or the stars in the sky is that an endless number of saints will be required to fully reflect the infinite facets of God's love. "Everyone is necessary in heaven," Joni exclaimed, "including you. For without you, some wonderful nuance of God's love (dare I say?) might not get reflected. And that can never be."

Yes, there will certainly be days when you'll wonder why you're taking up space on the planet. There will be days when Satan will insist your life isn't worth a dented fender on an old pickup.

Never believe it! God's plans for you reach through time into eternity. The Creator knew exactly what He was about when He drew you together, cell by cell, in the sacred darkness of your mother's womb.

David had it right. You *are* fearfully and wonderfully made.

—*L.L.*

no wasted days

He has a plan for me

All the days ordained for me
were written in your book
before one of them came to be.

PSALM 139:16

What a storm of emotions floods our souls when we're about to embark on a new phase of life! Anticipation, fear, hope, sadness, excitement, dread—they all crowd their way into our trembling hearts, like anxious homesteaders rushing to stake claims to a new frontier.

Take high school graduation, for instance. Twenty-five years ago this spring I marched across the platform at Beloit Memorial High to accept my diploma, thus marking the official end of one season of life and the beginning of another—a wholly unknown other. I still remember my conflicting emotions as I walked from one end of the dais to the other:

elation that I had completed my senior year,

worry over finding a summer job,

excitement about college,

sadness over leaving friends,

and thrills (competing with chills) over the idea of "finally living on my own."

I remember, too, the scene backstage as we seniors donned our caps and gowns and prepared to file out to our seats in the gymnasium. Jeannie Jabush, I recall, was crying. My friend Dimmie Collins was strutting his stuff for a camera-wielding lady admirer. One group of friends, arms draped around each other, laughed loudly and told jokes; another circle crowded together in a tight pack, whispering.

Everyone knew "this was it."

No more notes passed in study hall.

No more card games at lunchtime.

No more battling computerized Klingons on the starship *Enterprise* in phonetics lab while we were supposed to be practicing our Spanish (that's the one I would miss). Times were about to change forever, a truth made obvious by the lumps in our senior throats.

AN ANCHOR IN THE STORM

When you reach a watershed place in your life and your warring emotions make it difficult to choose between the myriad options before you, it's important to step back and get a firm grip on something solid, unchanging, and absolutely reliable. You need an anchor in the storm, a blazing bonfire in the night, a lofty mountain soaring in the middle of a vast and featureless plain. You need the rock-solid bearings declared by King David:

All the days ordained for me
were written in your book
before one of them came to be.

As David pondered his own uncertain future, he took great comfort in affirming that his all-knowing God could never be surprised or caught off-guard by anything that might happen. All of David's personal history—every day, every hour, every moment—was, quite literally, an open book to God.

But his great confidence arose from more than that. David didn't mean simply that God knew exactly how long he was going to live. The Hebrew word translated "ordained" *(yasar)* carries the idea of purpose, of a divine plan. It comes from the same root as the word translated "potter" and is used elsewhere to describe a craftsman who takes a bit of clay and skillfully shapes and molds it into a beautiful and functional work of art.

When David praised God that "all the days ordained for me were written in your book before one of them came to be," he meant that the Lord wanted him to live out a specific, divine purpose—a good purpose that God would be delighted to fulfill in him. The shepherd-king did not have to worry about accidentally missing out on God's best, nor did he have to struggle through life hoping against hope that he might somehow stumble upon the reason for his existence. No! God rejoices in displaying His power and glory in the lives of his children as they fulfill His divinely ordained purposes. David knew this; that's why his heart leaped at the thought that the Creator of the universe doubled as his personal potter. David exulted in the idea that a loving Craftsman delighted in molding and shaping him *uniquely* according to His sovereign will.

This extraordinary thought brought such comfort to David that he couldn't keep it out of his poetry:

> I cry out to God Most High,
>> to God, who fulfills his purpose for me.
>> (Psalm 57:2)

> The LORD will fulfill his purpose for me;
>> your love, O LORD, endures forever—
>> do not abandon the works of your hands.
>> (Psalm 138:8)

David banked on this truth in good times and bad, when he felt sure of God's direction and when he didn't. He lived with the growing conviction that as he placed his trust in the Lord, God would "fulfill His purpose" for him, regardless of the obstacles and in spite of the confusion.

That doesn't mean, of course, that David always got it *right* about the direction God wanted him to head. In his mature years, for example, David longed to build a temple where all Israel could worship Yahweh. After consulting a prophet of the Lord about this desire, he began assembling construction materials, lined up builders, and secured artisans. "I had it in my heart to build a house for the Name of the LORD my God," he later told his son Solomon (1 Chronicles 22:7). But God would not allow David to build the temple; instead he chose Solomon for that task. It was not God's purpose for David to erect Israel's house of worship.

So then, did David sin in his intense desire to build a temple for God? Never! As the Lord Himself told the youngest of Jesse's sons, "Because it was in your heart to build a temple for my Name, you did well to have this in your heart" (1 Kings 8:18). It might not be God's purpose for David to build the temple, but the Lord would work through even the king's unfulfilled desires to accomplish His divine plan. In fact, none of the king's preparations were wasted; Solomon made use of them all. God wastes nothing!

And now for the really good news: God wants to do for you what He did for David. Despite any impediments to the contrary, God has a purpose for your life that He longs to fulfill. The only thing He asks is that you trust Him.

No Matter What

Although my high school commencement brought a host of competing emotions to the surface, I didn't have to puzzle over one thing: my chosen course of study. Through the influence of Ray Schoenfield—wise and witty advisor to our school newspaper, *The Increscent*—I had decided during my junior year to major in journalism. Only once did I seriously consider changing directions. Bernie Barkin, my chemistry teacher and former basketball coach, offered to set up an interview with a large local company that offered full scholarships to engineering students who agreed to spend a few years with the firm after college graduation. I toyed with the idea, but in a few days I decided it wasn't for me. Ever since grade school I've been happily involved in some form of communications—writing, drama, speaking—and that's where my heart drew me.

Of course I know it's not that way for everyone. Many of my friends struggled for years to declare a major. And even once it *had* been declared, that didn't settle the matter. Some friends declared and then redeclared and then redeclared again. Nothing wrong with that—except that such uncertainty can wreak havoc with our sense of God's direction and control. We thought He wanted us one place, *but what if He doesn't? What if I make the wrong choice? Will that doom me to a lifetime of second best, to a generation of God's scowl?*

I think David would tell us, "Relax, friend! Listen, you are trusting God, aren't you? Well then, you have nothing to fear. Oh, I don't mean you should make these choices flippantly. No, choose as wisely as you know how. But if your heart's desire is to please God and you're walking closely with Him, you needn't worry about making 'the wrong choice.' He'll bring you around to the 'right' spot! Remember, He's made you for a purpose—and God always fulfills His purpose in the lives of His beloved children. So relax!"

In this regard I always think of Larry Libby, my dear friend, business partner, and co-author. Like me, Larry had aimed since high school toward a career in journalism. But as he neared graduation

from the University of Oregon, a problem arose that made him question God's purpose for his life. I'll let him tell the story from here.

> In my senior year I was barely passing my journalism
> major. In one key class, my professor, a very kindly man,
> called me in to talk. He made it clear I was a whisker
> away from failing his class (I hadn't handed in enough
> assignments or something). And he wanted to talk about
> my future and my career.
>
> My heart was pounding as I walked into his small
> office. All my plans seemed on the verge of collapse.
> "You know," he began, "if you were serious about jour-
> nalism, you really should be passing these classes. Are
> you certain you want to enter this field?"
>
> The past year had so shaken my confidence that I
> really had my doubts. "Well," I stammered, "I have done
> some thinking about pursuing some aspect of missions. I
> think I could get interested in becoming a missionary at
> some point."
>
> With visible relief, my professor seized on my com-
> ment. "I'll tell you what," he said slowly. "If you will
> promise me that you will *not* pursue a career in journal-
> ism, I will pass you. Otherwise, you will fail."
>
> I so promised, and under those conditions I passed his
> class and earned my degree. I really didn't think I had a
> future in journalism. I thought I was washed up as a writer.

But the Lord had other things in mind. He said to Larry, in effect, "*You* might think you're washed up, but *I* don't think you're washed up. As a matter of fact, I know right where I want you."

Larry spent the next year at Multnomah Bible College, where God used another professor, Bruce Wilkinson (founder of Walk Thru the Bible Ministries), to challenge him to consider a career in writing. Dr. Wilkinson was forever scribbling notes on Larry's papers, encouraging him to use and hone his writing gifts. Eventually he got Larry in the door at Multnomah Press, where my friend soon began working with many of evangelical Christianity's most influential authors. He's also written five warm and wise children's books of his own—not bad for someone who was told he had no future in writing!

You see, God really is committed to "fulfilling his purpose" for His own. In this case, Larry thought he'd become a missionary; his journalism professor *hoped* he'd become a missionary (or anything else that would prevent him from becoming a journalist); and God thought Larry would make an outstanding editor/writer of Christian books.

Guess who knew best?

(Postscript: After wrestling with his conscience, Larry is *not* giving back his journalism degree.)

SERVING YOUR GENERATION

The book of Acts offers a delightful perspective on David's life and career. In Acts 13:36 Dr. Luke tells us, "When David had served God's purpose in his own generation, he fell asleep."

At the top of its lungs, this verse shouts that it is possible for us to fulfill God's purpose in this life, right up to the moment of our death. Think of what is being said here! God gave David a specific purpose to fulfill in his generation, and David fulfilled it. Sure, the man stumbled. Yes, he made some monster mistakes. And no, he didn't always brim with confidence that God's hand was guiding and directing his life. (See Psalm 13.) But *through it all,* David trusted God to fulfill His good purpose in David's life. And He did!

Contrast that with the chilling verse found in Luke 7:30, where the good doctor reported, "But the Pharisees and experts in the law rejected God's purpose for themselves."

Rejected God's purpose for themselves? What does that mean? Doesn't Proverbs 19:21 say, "Many are the plans in a man's heart, but it is the LORD's purpose that prevails"? Doesn't God say, "My purpose will stand, and I will do all that I please" (Isaiah 46:10)? What does Luke mean, they "rejected God's purpose for themselves"?

He means, I think, that the only way to derail God's purpose for your life is to tear up the tracks yourself. The Pharisees and experts in the law of Jesus' day didn't miss God's best by accident. They didn't innocently amble off God's pathway and discover too late that they had arrived exactly where they didn't want to be. Luke says they "rejected" God's purposes for them—a deliberate, conscious, calculated decision to refuse God's will for their lives. Frightening thought!

So is it possible to reject God's purpose for ourselves? Is there a real danger that we, too, might not fulfill God's will for us? Yes—but *only* if we spit in God's face and scream, "NO!" But why would any of us want to do that? As the writer of Hebrews said, "Even though we speak like this, dear friends, we are confident of better things in your case—things that accompany salvation" (Hebrews 6:9).

No matter what those "things that accompany salvation" might be in your case, never forget that God has a specific purpose for you that He wishes to fulfill. He aims to bring it to completion, as He did with David, *and no mistake or confusing situation or accident or bad decision can prevent Him from accomplishing His goal.*

And what is His goal? The prophet Jeremiah said it like this: "'I know the plans I have for you,' declares the LORD, 'plans to prosper you and not to harm you, plans to give you hope and a future. Then you will call upon me and come and pray to me, and I will listen to you. You will seek me and find me when you seek me with all your heart'" (Jeremiah 29:11-13).

When you walk with God, you don't have to worry about wasted days. He has recorded each one of your days in His book, eons before you were born. At this very moment He invites you to fulfill His purposes as you trust Him. And you can live every day for the rest of your life in the full confidence that He will direct your way.

No matter what. No matter where.

—*S.H.*

always on his mind

I am continually in His thoughts

How precious to me are your thoughts, O God!

How vast is the sum of them!

Were I to count them,

they would outnumber the grains of sand.

When I awake,

I am still with you.

PSALM 139:17-18

What was it that struck David with such wonder? What lifted him to such praise? On the day he captured the words of Psalm 139:17-18— glad words that exult in God's limitless thoughts—what brought him such ecstasy?

I like to imagine him sitting on the shore of the Great Sea, away from the wars and politics and intrigues of office, listening to the pounding waves, running handfuls of warm, white sand between his fingers.

Some Bible scholars emphasize that David was overwhelmed by

the character and sheer number of God's thoughts. How innumerable and lofty, pure and wondrous they are! And without question, that is a subject to stagger the understanding. What kind of Designer, what kind of Mind, could have shaped trillions of multicolored suns scattered across the heavens like dust in the wind—yet paid such infinite attention to perfect little desert flowers so tiny you have to get down on your stomach even to see them? In the book of Romans, when Paul began to contemplate God's wisdom, it immediately threw all his circuit breakers. *Click. Click. Click.* Just that quickly, the great apostle was at a loss.

"Oh, the depth of the riches of the wisdom and knowledge of God!" he shouts. "How unsearchable his judgments, and his paths beyond tracing out!" (Romans 11:33).

You could certainly dig your hands through the sand on an endless beach and compare each grain to the thoughts of the great Creator God. He has thoughts about the past, the present, and the future. He has thoughts about wars and kings, presidents and armies. He ponders the sunsets on Mars, feels the surge of the great methane storms on Jupiter, and walks the icy canyons of Uranus. Yet at the same time, He tracks the path of a single ant across a sidewalk in Milwaukee. This is a God who thinks of countless trillions of things every moment—though He lives beyond the reckoning of time.

That's a lot to think about.

But just between you and me, I believe David had something a little different in mind when he wrote those words. Translator Ken Taylor may have captured it best in his *Living Bible* paraphrase.

How precious it is, Lord,
    to realize that you are thinking about me constantly!
I can't even count how many times a day
    your thoughts turn towards me.
And when I waken in the morning,
    you are still thinking of me!

The thoughts of God that so amazed David weren't just any thoughts passing through the Infinite Mind. They were thoughts about David! That whole shoreline of sand—dunes and rolling dunes of it as far as the eye could see or imagine—was filled with individual thoughts of God about *him*.

And whether you are prepared to believe it or not, He fills that same infinite shoreline with thoughts of you, as well. "How vast is the sum of them!"

A COIN OF LOVE

David thrilled to the idea that God was constantly thinking of him. At least, he did in *this* psalm. It doesn't take a very long tour through the Psalms, however, to note that sometimes the shepherd-king complained that God wasn't thinking *at all* about him: "How long, O LORD? Will you forget me forever?" (Psalm 13:1).

Like David, sometimes we're so stressed and beaten down and wrung out by circumstances that we don't *feel* as though He is thinking of us. Loving us. But He is, all the same.

The weight I felt on my chest as I lay in bed one September morning was *not* our burly orange tomcat (an animal with a perverse fondness for stretching out, sphinxlike, on my chest and staring at me through those smug slits of pale emerald). If it had been the cat, I could have shaken him off my comforter like a bad dream and begun my day feeling more or less normal.

But there was no cat, and the feeling of weight persisted as I dressed quietly in the semidarkness of the bedroom. Silent as a wraith in my still-sleeping household, I slipped into the kitchen, nuked a cup of instant coffee, and groped in the cupboard for my favorite, high-fat granola.

My limbs seemed leaden as I moved through my morning routine. Somehow I felt three miles behind in my day before I'd downed my first bite of breakfast.

I was involved in several projects at work that seemed to carry illogical, impossible deadlines. That's par for the course in the publishing business, but on that particular morning I took it all to heart.

Besides that, I seemed to be in a losing battle to walk with Christ. I knew very well the kind of life He wanted me to lead—and really, it was the kind of life I *wanted* to lead, too. But for whatever reason, I couldn't get on track. My "Christian walk" felt like wading in knee-deep peanut butter. Day by day, I seemed to be tangling myself in a web of impure thoughts and negative attitudes. (Never mind what they were. Just take it from me they didn't belong.)

Wasn't I ever going to make progress in this spiritual life thing?

Wasn't I ever going to please Him, or be of some minimal, moderate benefit to His kingdom?

If you had asked me that morning, "Does God love you?" I could have given you all the "right" answers. I knew the Scripture verses and the textbook replies. But I felt nothing in my heart. Nothing but a heaviness approximating the weight of a seventeen-pound tomcat.

Finished with my morning preparations, I grabbed my briefcase, double-checked my pocket for the right bus change, and started for the front door. Passing through the darkness of the curtained living room, I put my hand on the doorknob, about to exit into another day of riding the bench on God's "B" team.

I don't know why I happened to look back. But I will never forget what I saw.

It really wasn't much.

Just a tiny pool of molten gold on the carpet.

Forgetting my rush to catch the 6:50 express, I stared at the phenomenon. How curious! Obviously, a single stray beam from the newly risen sun was paying a call to our living room floor. Funny, I hadn't even realized the sun was up. But where had that bit of radiance come from? The rest of the house was dark—doors locked, blinds closed, curtains drawn. Somehow a playful, pencil-thin sliver of sunrise had found its way through some chink in curtain and blinds to touch the floor at my feet. There was no other light in the room. Just that one little disk, gleaming like a newly minted gold coin.

I set my briefcase down and went over to look at it. I walked around it. Touched it. Wondered at it. Somehow in that moment, it seemed like something more than an itinerant sunbeam. More than a curious trick of light. Just that quickly I felt the presence of the Lord. I knew with all my heart it was a calling card from God.

I knelt in the spot, letting the tiny light play across my face, like the touch of a golden finger. It was as if God were saying to me, "See this bright little coin on your carpet? I left it there. Just for you. If you will receive it, it's just one token of My love for you this morning. Go ahead now. You're in a hurry, aren't you? Grab your briefcase. Catch your bus. But, oh, if you could see what lies behind that little circle of light—*a blazing sun.* A white-hot stellar furnace of My love. Awesome in power. Enduring through the ages. Piercing time and space. More than you could begin to imagine or comprehend in an eternity. I don't love you for what you *do,* son, but for who you *are.* And you are Mine. Now, catch your bus!"

I don't remember if I caught the 6:50 that day. I don't remember if I made those work deadlines that had seemed so incredibly important when I first opened my eyes that morning. If I missed a few of them, I can testify that the stars did not fall from the heavens nor did the world cease spinning on its axis.

But in that moment, in that otherwise gray September, I accepted that bright little coin of His presence. I couldn't slip it into my pocket, but I tucked it into memory. I let that slender needle of radiance thread its way through the curtains and shutters of my heart.

I felt loved.

It may be that, right at this moment, you need to feel His love, too. So many changes have taken place in your life so quickly that the earth beneath your feet seems to wobble. You're excited about the green, broad horizons opening up before you, but it's an excitement tinged with fear. You'd give anything for your very own little "coin of love."

I can't promise you that God will minister to you exactly as He did to me that morning so long ago. I don't know how you best "feel" His love. *But He does love you!* I urge you to begin looking for that golden coin of your own—or is it silver? Whatever it looks like, God wants to give it to you, for He wants you to rest in His unchanging love. Maybe you just need to learn where to look for it.

He Was Just Thinking About You

Have you ever had a friend call just moments after he or she crossed your mind? And you say, "This is really strange. I was *just thinking about you*—and the phone rang!"

God was "just thinking about you" when you first opened your eyes this morning. He was "just thinking about you" when you walked into your first class today or punched in at the job. He was "just thinking about you" when you walked into the parking lot at sunset and the wind touched your hair.

"Ah," you say, "but how do I *know* the Lord is thinking about me, as you say? It's a pleasant concept, but I haven't seen all that much evidence of it."

The answer to that question, I believe, lies less in His capacity to express love than in our capacity to receive it. Many of us—however unintentionally—shut God out of our thoughts. We box Him out of our day. Compartmentalize Him out of our week. We become like that sad man in Psalm 10:4, of whom it was said, "In all his thoughts there is no room for God."

No room for God—the mighty Creator and Lord of the universe? No room for Christ—Savior, Brother, and King? How could He be shut out?

The fact is, the morning sun may rise in glorious splendor bathing your home, your neighborhood, and your city with rivers of majestic light. But if you're inside the house with all the windows curtained and all the blinds closed, how would you know it? How can you tell it isn't dark as midnight? You rely on your own poor, 100-watt artificial lights when great, silent oceans of illumination flood across your roof and beat against your windows like breakers.

If you want to experience the light, you have to open the blinds.

In my case, a single beam of sunlight found a tiny opening and shone through to my living room.

God, too, sends His little shafts of brightness into a busy life that crowds Him out. He leaves His bright gold coins as small tokens of a love so vast the vaults of heaven cannot contain it. Will you recognize those coins when you see them? Or will you hurry on by without taking time to notice?

When we were just boys, my cousin saw a tiny glint of light while playing in my grandfather's back pasture. He stopped to investigate and picked up a twenty-dollar gold piece that had most likely lain in that field for seventy years. We'd all played in that pasture since we could walk, but no one had seen anything like it. My cousin, however, had his eyes open that day and claimed the prize.

If God's loving thoughts toward us are like coins, what might these coins look like?

It might be a Bible verse, popping into your head without any logical reason or connection. *And what made you suddenly remember it?*

It might come in the form of a note or letter. A friend—or even your grandmother!—might say, "You've been on my mind the last couple of days. I've been praying for you." *Who prompted that person to pray for you—and then to tell you about it?*

It might be a line from a hymn or praise song that somehow weaves its way through your thoughts, speaking of God's care and concern for you. *Who pulled that musical thread through your crowded mind?*

Maybe it's a scene from a movie—a movie that has nothing whatsoever to do with Jesus. Yet some big screen moment moves you emotionally and you find yourself thinking about...Him. *How could thoughts of Jesus work their way unseen into a godless, Hollywood production?*

He might speak to you from an inscription on a calendar...or a rainbow arching a stormy horizon...or a red leaf floating through the muted light of an October afternoon...or the bright smile of a toddler.

You hear a whisper in the wind, a call in the pounding waves—a "still small voice" that says, *"Come to Me. Walk with Me."*

When David caught a glimpse, a fleeting realization of a God who thought about him constantly, he bowed low in wonder. He found himself confessing his sins and crying out for God's counsel and direction in his life (Psalm 139:23-24).

He didn't need to spend all day counting grains of sand. He just wanted to run on the beach with his King.

—L.L.

the end game for evil

He will right every wrong

> If only you would slay the wicked, O God!
>> Away from me, you bloodthirsty men!
> They speak of you with evil intent;
>> your adversaries misuse your name.
> Do I not hate those who hate you, O LORD,
>> and abhor those who rise up against you?
> I have nothing but hatred for them;
>> I count them my enemies.

PSALM 139:19-22

An unhappy observer of our decaying culture once remarked, "Idealism is what precedes experience; cynicism is what follows."[1] Conserva-

---

1. David T. Wolf, *1,911 Best Things Anybody Ever Said*, ed. Robert Byrne (New York: Fawcett Columbine, 1988), 236.

tive thinker William F. Buckley Jr., apparently agreed, for he quipped, "Idealism is fine, but as it approaches reality the cost becomes prohibitive."[2]

It's a good bet that both of these men, somewhere along the line, ran headlong into what theologians call "the problem of evil." In their younger days, they probably set out with high ideals, clear eyes, and limitless enthusiasm to conquer world hunger, alleviate human suffering, and usher in planetary peace. But sooner or later they discovered that not everyone shared their humanitarian concerns. For the first time, perhaps, they slammed facefirst into a flesh-and-blood example of human greed or prejudice or selfishness or hatred.

And they hit the "eject" button on their idealism.

The harsh truth is, we live in a world where evil—hateful, murderous, wanton, senseless *evil*—exists and even flourishes. Every day we read in the newspapers and hear on the radio and see on television countless reports of horrific human wickedness. As an experiment, I just walked down the street to pick up an afternoon edition of the local newspaper. Here is what I read:

- A New York bank official resigned amid billion-dollar scandal accusations.
- Virginia's governor announced a probe into charges that guards sexually abuse inmates at a women's prison.

---

2. William F. Buckley Jr., *The Portable Curmudgeon,* ed. Jon Winokur (New York: New American Library, 1987), 153.

- The Justice Department will investigate the fatal shooting of an African-American man by two white city police officers.
- Three law officers and a suspect were killed last night in a gun battle in Pleasanton, Texas.
- The Pakistani army ousted that nation's democratically elected leader, touching off concerns about control and use of nuclear weapons.

And all that was on the first two pages *alone,* on a slow news day!

Our world is in serious trouble, and most of it is caused by "man's inhumanity to man." That's important for us to remember, for while God wants us to launch out into the world where we are to act as salt and light (Matthew 5:13-16), he doesn't want us to forget what kind of a world it is. "I am sending you out like sheep among wolves," Jesus warned us (Matthew 10:16).

I think that's why David fires off an assault against the enemies of God toward the end of Psalm 139. He pleads with his Lord to wipe out the wicked, to destroy those who in both word and deed rebel against God. He says that he has "nothing but hatred" for these rebels and that he counts them his own mortal enemies.

Wow. We're not used to finding such a verbal blitzkrieg in Scripture. What are we to make of this passionate outburst? How are we to respond to such zealous emotions? Why did God put these verses in His Word, and what are we to learn and remember from them as we take our next few steps into the great adventure to which the Lord has called us?

LESSON ONE: JUDGMENT IS COMING

These days we tend to downplay the seriousness of sin. We make "mistakes," "miscalculations," or "serious errors in judgment"; we don't "do wrong" or "commit evil." We think of ourselves as basically good folk who occasionally make poor choices, not as people born in sin who often hurry to follow the desires of our corrupt hearts.

The psalmists, including David, saw things differently. The holiness and righteousness of God so filled their eyes and enflamed their hearts that they could not sit still to see His name profaned or His will defied. Perhaps you've experienced some of the same emotions when you've heard the name of Jesus casually defiled. C. S. Lewis wrote, "The ferocious parts of the Psalms serve as a reminder that there is in the world such a thing as wickedness, and that it…is hateful to God."[3]

Because God is holy, because He is infinitely righteous, He must judge sin. *All* sin. This is the consistent message of Scripture:

> But I tell you that men will have to give account on
> the day of judgment for every careless word they have
> spoken. (Matthew 12:36)

> God "will give to each person according to what he has
> done." To those who by persistence in doing good seek
> glory, honor and immortality, he will give eternal life.

---

3. C. S. Lewis, *Reflections on the Psalms* (New York: Harcourt Brace, 1964), 19, 33.

But for those who are self-seeking and who reject the
truth and follow evil, there will be wrath and anger.
(Romans 2:6-8)

God is just: He will pay back trouble to those who trouble
you and give relief to you who are troubled, and to us as
well.... They will be punished with everlasting destruction
and shut out from the presence of the Lord and from the
majesty of his power. (2 Thessalonians 1:6-7,9)

For we know him who said, "It is mine to avenge; I will
repay," and again, "The Lord will judge his people." It is
a dreadful thing to fall into the hands of the living God.
(Hebrews 10:30-31)

I am he who searches hearts and minds, and I will repay
each of you according to your deeds. (Revelation 2:23)

No one ultimately "gets away with" anything. There are no "perfect crimes." It is impossible to evade justice forever. David and the other psalmists and members of God's chorus remind us that sin is real, that God hates it, and that one day all evil will be destroyed and all offenders punished.

The apostle John spoke of a "great white throne" and of an awesome figure who sat upon it, from whom both earth and sky fled. John said he "saw the dead, great and small, standing before the throne, and books were opened. Another book was opened, which is the book of life. The dead were judged according to what they had done as recorded in the books" (Revelation 20:11-12). John said, "If anyone's name was not found written in the book of life, he was thrown into the lake of fire" (verse 15).

Note carefully that the only way to avoid such awful judgment is to have one's name written in this "book of life." The obvious question is, how can I be certain that *my* name appears in that all-important book? There is only one way: to place my faith in Jesus Christ, God's sinless Son, who died on the cross to pay for my sins and who rose again to bring me eternal life. As the Bible says, "God made him [Jesus] who had no sin to be sin for us, so that in him we might become the righteousness of God" (2 Corinthians 5:21).

I wonder, is your name written in the book of life? Have you placed your faith in Jesus? Psalm 139 reminds us that a day of certain judgment is coming, and the New Testament declares that, through Jesus, we can steer clear of God's wrath when it comes.

Lesson Two: God Decides When and How

On the classic '70s television show *Sanford and Son,* the mean-tempered Aunt Esther took great delight in threatening divine judgment on the wayward Fred Sanford. Occasionally, when the junk king had had enough, he would threaten his own judgment as he shook his fist and shouted, "Vengeance may be the Lord's, but *I'm the Lord's helper!*"

It made for a funny bit, but as theology it stank. When it comes to judgment, God doesn't need our help. He alone decides its time and manner:

> It is mine to avenge; I will repay.
>> In due time their foot will slip;
> their day of disaster is near
>> and their doom rushes upon them.
>>> (Deuteronomy 32:35)

> The Lord laughs at the wicked,
>> for he knows their day is coming. (Psalm 37:13)

We simply don't know enough to determine how or when human evil should be punished. God alone perceives the thoughts and motives of the heart, and He alone determines when His hand of judgment must fall. The apostle Paul put it like this: "The sins of some men are obvious, reaching the place of judgment ahead of them; the sins of others trail behind them" (1 Timothy 5:24). In other words, some sins receive a partial judgment even in this life, while others await sentencing for the final day of God's wrath. And only the Lord makes those determinations.

If God judged all sin immediately, who among us would be left on the planet? But if He never punished anyone before the end, who would take His warnings seriously? So in His grace God punishes some now and leaves the rest for later.

Of course we like it better when the sins of others reach "the place of judgment ahead of them." I, for one, love to read stories about how stupid criminals get caught. Like these incidents reported on the Net:

> Two men tried to pull the front off a cash machine by running a chain from the machine to the bumper of their pickup truck. Instead of pulling the front panel off the machine, however, they pulled the bumper off their truck. Scared, they left the scene and drove home. With the chain still attached to the machine. With their bumper still attached to the chain. With their vehicle's license plate still attached to the bumper.

> When a man attempted to siphon gasoline from a motor home parked on a Seattle street, he got much more than he bargained for. Police arrived at the scene to find an ill man curled up next to the vehicle. Police said the man admitted to trying to steal gasoline, but plugged his hose into the motor home's sewage tank by mistake. The owner of the vehicle declined to press charges, saying it was the best laugh he'd ever had.

> Edilber Guimaraes, 19, was arrested in Belo Horizonte, Brazil, for attempted theft at a glue factory. As Guimaraes stopped to sniff some of the glue he was stealing, he knocked over two large cans, spilling their contents. When police arrived at the factory, Guimaraes was sitting immobile, glued to the floor.

And then there's this final story. Although it sounds apocryphal to me, it's just too choice to leave out:

> A Charlotte, North Carolina man, having purchased a case of rare, very expensive cigars, insured them against *fire*. Within a month, having smoked his entire stockpile of fabulous cigars, and having yet to pay a single premium, the man filed a claim against the insurance company, stating that he had lost the cigars in "a series of small fires."
>
> The insurance company refused to pay, citing the obvious reason that the man had consumed the cigars in a normal fashion. The man sued AND WON!
>
> The ruling judge stated that since the man held a policy from the company in which it warranted that the cigars were insurable, and also guaranteed that it would insure the cigars against fire—without defining what it considered to be "unacceptable fire"—it was obligated to compensate the insured for his loss. Rather than endure a lengthy and costly appeals process, the insurance company paid the man $15,000 for the rare cigars he lost in "the fires."

This part of the story outraged me when I first read it. But as Paul says, "the sins of some men are obvious, reaching the place of judgment ahead of them." Do they ever!

After the man cashed his check, however, the insurance company had him arrested on twenty-four counts of arson! With his own insurance claim and testimony from the previous case being used as evidence against him, the man was convicted of intentionally burning the rare cigars. He was sentenced to twenty-four consecutive one-year terms!

In His parable of the weeds Jesus told us that both good and evil will grow together until the final harvest (Matthew 13:24-30). At that time God will sort one from the other and reward the former while burning the latter. We may wish that He would act sooner to rid the world of sin, but as Peter reminds us,

> But do not forget this one thing, dear friends: With the Lord a day is like a thousand years, and a thousand years are like a day. The Lord is not slow in keeping his promise, as some understand slowness. He is patient with you, not wanting anyone to perish, but everyone to come to repentance. (2 Peter 3:8-9)

LESSON THREE: BE POSITIVE (BUT WISE)

So what are we to do in the meanwhile? How are we to live in this world that's headed for judgment? Jesus tells us to be salt—a preservative that adds flavor to life. He tells us to be light—a beacon of hope in the darkness. He tells us to actively look for ways to serve others until He returns (Luke 19:13).

And He tells us to be wise.

Immediately after He warned us that "I am sending you out like sheep among wolves," He added, "Therefore be as shrewd as snakes and as innocent as doves" (Matthew 10:16). We cannot allow the evil of the world to snuff out our dreams for making that world a better place, but neither can we afford to enter the battle without first putting on some heavy armor. You and I are to "be wise in the way you act toward outsiders; make the most of every opportunity" (Colossians 4:5). How wise? Shrewd as snakes, Jesus says, because "The people of this world are more shrewd in dealing with their own kind than are the people of the light" (Luke 16:8).

We must be wise!

And when we tap into the storehouses of divine wisdom that are offered to us without limit or measure (James 1:5), we will discover that a biblical idealism can instruct and energize us to live with great joy and effectiveness in a world groaning under the burden of sin. For then we will truly be "Christ's ambassadors," as Paul pictures us in 2 Corinthians 5:20.

And that's a job description for the heartiest idealist among us.

—*S.H.*

the most important thing in the world

Yielding my will to His

Search me, O God, and know my heart;

test me and know my anxious thoughts.

See if there is any offensive way in me.

PSALM 139:23-24

What's the most important thing in the world to you? When God looks at your life and the decisions you make about it, what would you like Him to say?

There's no question what most powerfully gripped the heart of David; he left no doubt about what he considered the most important thing in the world. In Psalm 139 the sweet psalmist of Israel made it clear that he desired nothing less than conformity to God's will. David longed to walk in step with God's Spirit, to desire what his Lord desired and to cherish what He cherished. He wanted God's will and his will to flow in the same channel and toward the same great sea.

Sounds wonderful, doesn't it? But David recognized he had to overcome one enormous problem if he were to gain this greatest desire of his heart. For while in the deepest part of his soul he longed to yield his will to the will of God, he knew by experience that a traitor lived within. He had to admit that there might be an "offensive way" in him, that "surely I was sinful at birth, sinful from the time my mother conceived me" (Psalm 51:5). He knew he tended to do exactly the *opposite* of what he really wanted to do.

Centuries later the apostle Paul would restate the problem like this: "I do not understand what I do. For what I want to do I do not do, but what I hate I do.... I know that nothing good lives in me, that is, in my sinful nature. For I have the desire to do what is good, but I cannot carry it out. For what I do is not the good I want to do; no, the evil I do not want to do—this I keep on doing" (Romans 7:15, 18-19). Jesus put it even more simply: "The spirit is willing, but the body is weak" (Matthew 26:41).

What a terrible dilemma! Supposing that you've already come to trust in God through faith in His Son, Jesus Christ—what can you do *now* to ensure that your will lines up with His will? What can you do to resist the downward pull of your fallen human nature? It's an especially crucial question as you prepare to make choices that will shape the rest of your life.

KEEP ON SEARCHING, LORD!

If following God's will is the most important thing in the world to you, let me suggest that you imitate David's example in Psalm 139. As he came to the close of that wonderful song, he uttered a wise and sincere prayer:

> *Search me, O God, and know my heart;*
> *test me and know my anxious thoughts.*
> *See if there is any offensive way in me.*

In verse one of his song, David declared that God *had* searched him and that He *did* know him. So why pray in verse 23 that the Lord *would* search him and know him?

Why? Because David craves an ongoing, dynamic relationship with God in which his Lord is constantly in touch with him. David asks Yahweh to search him and know him so that David might benefit from the search. The king wants to know what God sees when He probes David's secret longings and hidden motivations. The king is wise enough to know that what he *thinks* are his real desires and motivations often *aren't*. But God could see clearly through the fog of David's misty human nature even when the king couldn't.

The summer after my first year of seminary, I hoped to do an internship at a local church. But where to find a suitable position? In my college days I found the competition fierce for a newspaper internship. So this time around I decided to send out inquiries to seven interested churches. Eventually the choice narrowed to two: a large

Presbyterian church in Anchorage, Alaska, and a small Baptist church in Estherville, Iowa. Both seemed to have strong ministries and both asked me to come. I hadn't expected this; all along I thought I would be happy to get a single invitation out of my seven inquiries. Which of these two solid opportunities should I choose?

I struggled with my decision for a long time. I spoke with leaders of one congregation, then the other. And still the choice didn't seem clear. *What was I to do?*

I tried to sort out my motives. I attempted to uncover any hidden desires. I wanted to make sure that I made a wise choice that pleased my heavenly Father, one that lined up with His will. But after days of intense pondering, I still wasn't sure. My own heart seemed a mystery to me.

Finally I chose the small Baptist church in Iowa. Two primary considerations tipped the scales:

- Since the Iowa church was the smaller of the two, I couldn't be choosing it for the glory of the position.
- Since I really wanted to see Alaska, I shouldn't choose the Anchorage church for fear that my motivations might be tainted.

I had a wonderful time that summer with the good people of Union Baptist Church, and God seemed to bless our efforts together. But in the succeeding years I have concluded that my decision-making process left a great deal to be desired. I had chosen Iowa primarily on the basis of *negative* criteria. That is, I feared I could be choosing the

Alaska option because it might afford a more "prestigious" position and because the state itself beckoned with tantalizing mysteries foreign to Iowa. Because I didn't want to make my choice based on possible "wrong" motivations (even though I wasn't at all sure I had any), I wound up in Iowa.

What a puzzle our own heart is to us! Even when we want to do the "right" thing, the thing that will most please and delight our heavenly Father, we often get lost in the murky shadows of hidden motives. No wonder Jeremiah wrote, "The heart is deceitful above all things and beyond cure. Who can understand it?" (Jeremiah 17:9). No one—except God! We can be eternally grateful that the prophet added, "I the LORD search the heart and examine the mind, to reward a man according to his conduct, according to what his deeds deserve" (Jeremiah 17:10).

To be frank, I don't remember if I asked God to "search me and know my heart" before I decided where to spend that summer so long ago. By His grace He used me in Iowa. But could He have used me just as much in Alaska? Might He have been just as pleased to hone my ministry skills in Anchorage even as I enjoyed a new adventure in a breathtaking part of His creation? Today I wonder whether I might not have bought into the lie that says, "If you really want it, it couldn't possibly be God's will for you."

If I had the same choice to make today, would I end up instead in the forty-ninth state? Perhaps. (And I might have been mauled by a polar bear too.) Yet wherever I might land in the remaining days of my life, I hope I will always first ask God to "search me and know my heart." He knows it so much better than I do—and He knows where to direct it so much better than I ever will.

TESTS AND ANXIOUS THOUGHTS

David asks not only that God would search his heart but also that He would "test" him and know his "anxious thoughts." The first time I considered this verse, it struck me how often tests are connected with anxious thoughts!

When I was a college sophomore in Eau Claire, Wisconsin, I took an incomplete in a physics class because the course final was scheduled for the same day as my brother's wedding in Boston, Massachusetts. I had ten weeks to make up the final, and let's just say I didn't maximize that time. All right, let's be honest: I didn't crack a book until the night before the test.

You just can't *do* that in physics and expect to get away with it. The more I studied my notes and textbooks, the more anxious I became. I remembered *none* of the material. Zip. It looked like hieroglyphics to me. And it didn't get much better as the clock continued to wind toward test time. My anxiety continued to mount.

During the exam I vaguely recalled how to solve the equations, but I was far from sure. I handed in my work, then waited a week to get my grade. When I walked into my professor's office to see whether I just might have squeaked by, he pivoted slowly on his swivel chair, pushed his glasses back up on his nose, stared at me for a moment with his bright, intense eyes, and said, "Mr. Halliday, *I am appalled at you.*"

One question answered.

Tests have a way of making us anxious. That is, most tests do. Happily, the kind of test David has in mind produces exactly the opposite effect. He asks God to test him and "know" his "anxious thoughts" *in order that his anxiety might decrease.* This divine testing didn't make David anxious but was intended to uncover the anxiety David already felt so that it might be eliminated.

All of us feel anxious from time to time. The fear of the unknown, worrying about what "might" happen, dreading an approaching event or major change—all these can make our hearts quake and our spirits shrink. And often we don't even know why we feel as we do. Where did that lump in our throat come from? Why do our hands shake? What is causing that dread that makes our heart flutter?

When David felt such anxiety, he prayed to his loving Lord, "test me and know my anxious thoughts." Maybe he said something like this:

> *Lord, I'm frightened. I dread tomorrow—and I'm not even*
> *sure why. My hands shake, my voice quakes, my legs feel*
> *like they're going to buckle. And I can't even explain to my*
> *friends what's happening.*
>
> *O my God, test me! Show me where this fear comes*
> *from. You know me better than I know myself, and I need*
> *some of that heavenly insight right now. Know my anxious*
> *thoughts, O God. And pour into me Your amazing peace.*

Do you need God's peace today? Does a new phase of life or a major decision fill your heart with anxiety? Does fear, even an irrational fear, stalk you in the night or hunt you in the day?

If so, David counsels you to bring your fears to God. Say to Him, "test me and know my anxious thoughts." Cast yourself on His grace and mercy and remember how much He cares for you (1 Peter 5:7). Bring all of your anxious thoughts, whatever they may be, to His loving attention, and thank Him for hearing you and promising to shower you with His peace (Philippians 4:6-7).

Many have been the times I have asked for God's peace when my heart trembled with anxiety. My first year of college, for example, I left home with no permanent place to stay. All the dormitories on campus had been filled, and I didn't know of any accommodations close to school. At the proverbial "last minute," Ron Anderson, the assistant pastor at my home church, arranged for me to stay at the home of his mother, who lived twenty-one miles from the campus.

As I pulled out of my parents' driveway to begin the four-hour drive to my new life as a college student, anxiety tightened like a vise. Certainly, excitement ruled. But what awaited me up north? What kind of situation had I gotten myself into? I had never met Mrs. Anderson, never even talked to her. And yet I was going to stay at her house?

I had been told that my host would not be at home when I arrived, but that I would find the key to the back door in a certain spot. I was to let myself in and make myself at home. *Really?*

Late that afternoon I found the hidden key. It turned easily in the lock, the heavy door swung open, and I quickly brought my few things inside. So this was...home? It didn't feel like it. Doubts continued to harass me until I saw the handwritten note on the kitchen table. "Dear Steve," it read in grandmotherly style, "I'm glad you're here! Make yourself at home. And you'll find some goodies in the freezer. Help yourself! I'll be back in a few days. (signed) Adelia Anderson."

I located the freezer and walked toward it. I cracked open the lid—and was startled by what I saw inside. There weren't "a few goodies," as the note declared. There appeared to be vast, unending mounds of them—doughnuts, cookies, bars, cakes, brownies, pies, muffins—all with handwritten notes attached, all addressed specifically to *me*.

My anxieties about starting college and finding a permanent place to live didn't disappear immediately, but in that moment they certainly did abate. God had worked beforehand, through one of His choice servants, to quiet my fears and speak peace to my anxious heart.

He wants to do the same for you. I don't know how God might be working beforehand to quiet your heart and replace your fretfulness with His peace, but I'm certain He is. You may not even know what lies deep in your heart, what secret motivations and desires prod you to do one thing and not another. No matter. All He asks is that you tell him about your fears and invite Him to test you and know your anxious thoughts. Call on Him to search you, to know your heart, to see if there is any "offensive way" in you—and if there is, determine now to yield it to Him so that His will can remain the most important thing in the world to you.

When you make these prayers your own, He takes over. Maybe He'll bring a Mrs. Anderson into your life. And maybe He won't.

But just the same, I know He's got some goodies for you. Heaping mounds of them, with a loving note attached to each delicious package.

—*S.H.*

trailhead to eternity

In search of the "way everlasting"

Lead me in the way everlasting.

PSALM 139:24

On a gray, humid afternoon a number of years ago, my family and I waited for over forty-five minutes to ride the Wild Waters Raft Excursion at Six Flags Over Georgia.

It was a bust.

The circular, metal rafts slid along a shallow, man-made river, past a synthetic jungle, artificial rocks, and under a fake waterfall.

Where were the "wild" waters? *Mild* would have described it better. The gentle rocking motion might have put a baby to sleep. I've experienced more adrenaline trying to put my tomcat out at night. The ride lasted just a few minutes, culminating with a sopping shower under a tepid waterfall.

Uh-huh. Yippee. What a rush.

Some years later, my teenage son and I decided to let ourselves in on the Real Thing. We joined a raft tour down the lower Deschutes

River in central Oregon, a nationally designated "wild and scenic river."

Before we climbed into the raft, our professional guide (a lean, aging hippie) cheerfully assured us that he was certified in swift water rescue, first aid, and CPR. Such comfort!

Six others joined us in our boat. Two chunky, wide-shouldered brothers claimed the front seats, left and right, armed with lethal looking Super-Soakers and barely suppressed grins.

It was a dry-country summer morning, without a hint of haze. The sun climbed a cloudless sky of deepest blue. Our ride began swiftly as the crystal clear current shot us out into mid-river. My son and I exchanged a glance and a wink, as if to say, "Well, here goes!"

Gaining speed, we swept past rolling hills, carpeted with tawny summer grass and dotted with juniper. Here and there an ancient ponderosa pine clung impossibly to a sheer cliff face or rocky outcropping.

Suddenly we ran out of time to admire scenery. The water just ahead of us looked distinctly *white*. And loud! That's the way it is with the Deschutes. Within a few hundred yards, the river may change in character from Class I to Class IV rapids—tossing in a few Class V rapids for variety. As the day sped by, we made our acquaintance with a dizzying succession of storied rapids with names like Wapinitia, Devil's Hole, Box Car, Surf City, Oak Springs, White River, and Upper and Lower Elevators.

We plunged. Lurched. Soared. Gasped. Yelled. Laughed. When our guide shouted "paddle left" or "paddle right," we stroked like fury, showering ourselves with clean, icy water. Our two big Mafia hit men in the front took it upon themselves to soak other rafting parties who had the nerve to remain dry. Our hippie guide grinned like a demon, his shoulder-length gray hair flying behind him. The way he whooped and hollered, you would have thought it was his first trip rather than his ten thousandth. Through it all, our hearts pounded with a mixture of terror and sheer joy. *What a trip! What a day!*

Downstream we caught our breath on quiet stretches where the river glided like green glass through virgin, sun-baked Indian lands. Then—it was off to the races again!

After such an intimate encounter with the Deschutes, can you imagine my son and me standing in line again to ride the "Wild Waters Raft Excursion" in Georgia? No chance! How dull and bland that would be. How could we enjoy someone's poor synthetic idea of a raft ride after we had tasted the hilarity and excitement of the genuine article?

I could be wrong, but I sense the same sort of question hovering behind the closing words of David's prayer in Psalm 139.

Don't Let Me Miss It!

Just before he gets up from his knees, the son of Jesse looks up into the heavens and whispers a poignant postscript:

And Lord, please lead me in the way everlasting.

What did he mean by that? What was going on in his heart at that moment? How would David have understood that phrase, "the way everlasting"?

In the Hebrew language, the word translated "way" can also mean a road or a journey. Years later, David's own son would write, "There is a way that seems right to a man, but in the end it leads to death" (Proverbs 14:12).

In other words, you can *think* you're on the right path, the trail that leads to happiness and fulfillment and success in life, only to discover you're on a dead end—and that you've missed all your heart really desired.

David understood that his life was constantly being pulled in one of two directions. There was God's direction for his life—"the way everlasting"—and there was the sinful, selfish direction for his life. Sadly, David would take the wrong road on a number of occasions, to his deep sorrow and regret. Yet down at the core of his being, he craved God's path, God's plan, God's best. He longed for the road with the stamp of eternity upon it. He had walked life's pathway with the very Lord of the universe, and he didn't want any cheap knockoffs or artificial substitutes. He had thrilled to the "way everlasting" and didn't want anything less.

Lead me, Lord! Lead me in the way everlasting. Without Your help, I might miss the path and end up wasting my life.

David had tasted the Lord's courage and power as a teenager, when he stood looking up at a nine-foot giant in the Valley of Elah. What had he said that day as he stood in the monster's shadow? "You come against me with sword and spear and javelin, but I come against you in the name of the LORD Almighty, the God of the armies of

Israel, whom you have defied.... The battle is the LORD's!" (1 Samuel 17:45,47).

David had tasted the Lord's goodness (Psalm 34:8)—he remembered the wild, sweet tang on his tongue—that made every other flavor taste like plaster of Paris. He had rafted on the furious, white waters of God's "river of delights." He had found refuge in the shadow of God's wings—like cool shade on a parched afternoon. He had feasted in the abundance of God's house. He had plunged his head into the bracing waters of the fountain of life, his eyes filled with light beyond the visible spectrum (Psalm 36:7-9). He had sampled "eternal pleasures" out of God's right hand (Psalm 16:11).

At one point he groped for words to tell the Lord what his experience meant to him. He compared it to the most festive, joy-filled occasion he could think of: a riotous party hosted by a farming community after an especially bountiful harvest.

"Lord," he said, "You have filled my heart with greater joy than when their grain and new wine abound" (Psalm 4:7). In other words, they can plunge their hands into the mountains of golden grain, kill the fatted calf, party until dawn, and tank up on the fruit of the vine. But they won't be as happy as I am right now!

Deep down, David sensed that no luxury, no man-created pleasure, no man-centered accomplishment could ever *touch* the thrill of running along God's path. Kingly riches and wine, women, and song might entertain and provide some temporary distraction, but it could never scratch where he itched in the deep places of his soul.

Thoughts like those aren't easy to put into words. I remember trying to do it myself, as an eighth grader.

A Fear of the Shallows

I sat on a metal folding chair in our church's stark white "inquiry room," looking into the calm, somewhat puzzled face of Ed Hoberg. He wasn't quite sure what to say.

"Well, my brother," he began, "what can I do for you?"

I had just responded to Pastor Williams's invitation at the end of his sermon. I had taken that infinitely long walk down the aisle of River Road Baptist Church in front of family, school friends, and strangers because—well, because I felt I had to.

Ed, an old family friend, knew I was already a Christian. So why had I responded to the appeal? He probably thought I lacked assurance of my salvation.

But that wasn't it.

How could I describe—how could I tell him about—well, what was it? A vision? A dream? A nagging fear? A warning from God?

"I dunno," I stammered. "I just have this fear."

Ed wisely said nothing, waiting for me to explain.

"I have this picture…in my mind," I began, hating the way this was sounding. But now I was committed; I had to plunge ahead. "I see myself as an old guy—a middle-aged man—years and years from now, and…it isn't good. My life is shallow."

I really did see it, that future day. I saw myself through a mist, walking by a huge body of water—a lake or an ocean. The water invited swimming—out, out, into the blue depths. But I wouldn't go. I wouldn't get wet. I would walk only along the edge, where a tiny bit of water lapped at my feet. I saw myself walking into the distance, always in the shallows, always with one foot in the water and one foot on the land.

The thought made me shudder. To think of living your life—the one life God has given you on this planet—and never venturing anything for Him! Never taking risks. Never stepping out. Never testing your faith. Never experiencing the surge of His power, the bite of danger, the exhilaration of His provision. What a colossal waste!

I looked up at Ed's kind, uncomprehending face, feeling that tightness of throat that always precedes tears. I hadn't wanted *that* to happen, either. "I don't want my life to be that way," I told him. "I don't want to always be in the shallow part. I…want to go deep…with the Lord."

I didn't know how else to say it, and I'm not sure Ed ever really understood. But that good, quiet deacon put a big hand on my knee and began to pray for God's peace and God's best in my life.

I Want My Life to Count

I believe David worried about missing the everlasting way long before I did. About getting caught up in all the glitz and glamour and glitter of this temporary world and forgetting the true meaning of life. In Psalm 39, he described those fears burning like a fire in his gut. Finally he cried aloud to God:

> Lord, help me to realize how brief my time on earth will be. Help me to know that I am here for but a moment more. My life is no longer than my hand! My whole lifetime is but a moment to you. Proud man! Frail as breath! A shadow! And all his busy rushing ends in nothing. He heaps up riches for someone else to spend. And so, Lord, my only hope is in you. Save me from being overpowered by my sins. (Psalm 39:4-8, TLB)

What a great prayer! David was saying, "Oh Lord, my life is so short. Don't let me waste it! Don't let me get caught up in stuff that won't matter two seconds after I close my eyes in death or You return to call me into the clouds. Show me how brief this life is. Show me how short these days are alongside eternity!"

I've prayed such words, too. *Lord, I want my life to count. I want to walk in the everlasting way right now. I don't want my life's works burned up in Your presence. I have tasted You in Your glory and splendor; don't let me go back, Lord, to foolishness and selfishness.*

Many high school students across America felt those emotions on hearing the news about how young Cassie Bernall met her Lord. Cassie had only begun her walk with Christ when a suicidal gunman at Columbine High School cut her life short with a bullet to the head.

"Do you believe in God?"

An instant's pause. A life flashing before her eyes. A quick decision and a calm answer. "Yes, I do believe in God."

And then it was over.

Cassie had that one crowning opportunity to proclaim her Savior and King, and then she found herself in eternity. Yet what an impact that one act of courage had! Thousands of Christian teens have been stirred and challenged to the core by that momentary encounter in a school library-turned-mortuary.

Cassie didn't miss it. Her feet had found "the way everlasting," and she kept to that path even with her life on the line. A tragedy, yes. She died, but not in vain! Many, many other feet have found the path of life because of her courage.

I pray that my son, now launched in his first year of college, will remember that difference. I pray that he will never trade the roar and rush of clean, white water under a bright desert sky for a fake river in an urban amusement park.

I pray for you, too—you who have read through the pages of this small book and now find yourself peering into a mysterious, uncharted future.

Real adventures await on "the everlasting way." Don't accept any substitute.

—L.L.